Do thou give heed to our prayers; be with us in this mystic function. Be thou present to the pious labors of thy servants, and to us who implore thy mercy. May thy Holy Spirit, in the overflowing fulness of His sevenfold grace, come down on this thy church … consecrate this church of thine by the unceasing outpouring of thy hallowing virtue

+ An Ancient Invocation +

SEVEN SPIRITS BURNING

by JOHN CROWDER

Sons of Thunder Ministries & Publications
Santa Cruz, California

Seven Spirits Burning by John Crowder
Published by Sons of Thunder Ministries & Publications
P.O. Box 3591
Santa Cruz, CA 95063

www.thenewmystics.com
Phone: **1-877-343-3245**
Email: info@thenewmystics.org

Library of Congress Catalog Number: 2010915410
International Standard Book Number: 0-977082628

Printed in the United States of America

9 8 7 6 5 4 3 2

To Holy Spirit ...
I'm glad you know what you're doing.

+ CONTENTS

+ TRANSLATION INDEX

In the following chapters, we will draw from multiple translations of the scriptures. The author has accumulated upward of 150 versions in English to date, and chosen some of the best here to accurately convey a robust understanding of scripture. A number of these are rare and out of print. We actively encourage you to begin your own translation library for a deeper drink of the pure, undiluted gospel!

An explanation of abbreviations

The translations used in this book can be identified by the following codes:

AKJV – *American King James Version* (Public Domain as of 1999). Michael Peter "Stone" Engelbrite.
AMP – *The Amplified Bible* (Grand Rapids: Zondervan Publishing House and The Lockman Foundation, 1954, 1958, 1962, 1964, 1965, 1987). Frances Siewert.
ARTB – *Ancient Roots Translinear Bible* (Fenton, MO: ARTB Publishing, 2006). A. Frances Werner.
BAS – *The New Testament in Basic English* (New York: Cambridge University Press, 1941).
CJB – *Complete Jewish Bible* (Clarksville, MD: Jewish New Testament Publications, Inc., 1998). David Stern.
DAR – *The Holy Scriptures: A Translation from the Original Languages* (Essex: Saville Street Distribution, 2006). John Darby.
DEW – *Praise-Songs of Israel: A Rendering of the Book of Psalms* (New York: Funk and Wagnalls, 1884). John DeWitt.
DIS – *The Distilled Bible: New Testament* (Stone Mountain, GA: P. Benjamin Publishers, 1980). Roy Greenhill.
DRB – *Douay-Rheims Bible 1582-1609* (Fitzwilliam, NH: Loreto Publications, 2007).
ESV – *The English Standard Version Bible: Containing the Old and New Testaments with Apocrypha* (Oxford: Oxford University Press, 2009).

TRANSLATION INDEX

GWT – *God's Word Translation* (Holiday, FL: Green Key Books, 1995, 2003).

ISV – *International Standard Version* (Yorba Linda, CA: Davidson Press, 1998).

KJV – *The Holy Bible King James Version: 1611 Edition.*

KNOX – *The New Testament of our Lord and Saviour Jesus Christ* (Springfield: Templegate Publishers, 1945). Ronald A. Knox.

MOF – *The Bible: James Moffatt Translation* (San Francisco: Harper Collins, 1922/1994). James Moffatt.

MSG – *The Message* (Colorado Springs: NavPress Publishing Group, 2005 ed.). Eugene Peterson.

NAB – *The New American Bible* (Grand Rapids: Catholic World Press and World Publishing, 1970).

NEB – *The New English Bible: New Testament* (New York: Oxford and Cambridge University Press, 1961).

NIV – *The Holy Bible, New International Version* (Grand Rapids: The Zondervan Corporation, 1973, 1978, 1984). International Bible Society.

NKJV – *New King James Version* (Thomas Nelson Publishers, 1982).

NLT – *New Living Translation* (Wheaton: Tyndale House Publishers, 1996, 2004, 2007).

NRSV – *New Revised Standard Version Bible* (Division of Christian Education of the National Council of the Churches of Christ, 1989).

PHI – *The New Testament in Modern English* (New York: The Macmillan Co., 1962). J.B. Phillips.

RSV – *The Holy Bible Revised Standard Version* (New York: Thomas Nelson & Sons, 1952).

TCNT – *The Twentieth Century New Testament* (New York/Chicago/Toronto: Fleming H. Revell Company).

WEY – *The New Testament in Modern Speech* (New York: Harper and Row Publishers, Inc., 1903). Richard Francis Weymouth.

The author has emphasized some scripture texts in bold lettering. Verses listed without translation references are partially quoted or inferred.

+ Author's Note
A Christocentric Pentecost

Since the advent of the modern charismatic movement, there has been a much-needed focus on the operations of Holy Spirit in the church. Yet apart from a clear revelation of grace, we have drifted the way of religionists in our attempts to purchase this priceless oil.

The Lord is now restoring a *Christocentric pneumatology* to the church. That is, a Christ-centered theology of Holy Spirit. We are about to rediscover the simple source ... that the complete inexhaustible entirety of the Godhead was poured out through the broken body of the Son. For according to the apostle Paul, *by our union with Christ, we are filled with it.*

This is the effortless scandal of grace.

+ INTRODUCTION
THE PERSON OF HOLY SPIRIT

From the onset, we come into this subject curious, confused or downright befuddled at the topic of *seven* Spirits. You have St. John and his vivid mystical imagery to thank for that. In describing celestial spheres and shadows of things to come, a daunting task is presented. Bible commentator William Barclay is right in saying, "all apocalyptic literature is necessarily cryptic. It is continually attempting to describe the indescribable, to say the unsayable, to paint the unpaintable."[1]

We may not analytically understand all the archetypes and metaphors of prophetic literature. However, we do have intimate *fellowship with the Mystery*. The Mystery is a person. And every enigma aims only to draw us into the revelation of Him.

This book is about the operations and personality of Holy Spirit. To understand Holy Spirit, we look at the person of Christ. And in seeing Christ, we see the heart of the Father.

Holy Spirit is the Spirit of Jesus. He is not an impersonal force, but rather our Friend, Comforter, Counselor, Guide, Teacher and constant Helper.

As the Paraclete, He empowers us to live a victorious life as believers, doing the work of ministry through us: preaching the gospel, healing the sick, raising the dead and exorcizing the demonic. He builds the Kingdom through us. He quickens us in the many various callings

---

[1] William Barclay, *The Daily Study Bible Series: The Revelation of John, Vol. 1* (Philadelphia: Westminster Press, 1976), 31.

and vocations to which believers attend in the marketplace – whether media, government, education, medical professions, the arts, the financial or technology sector. Whatever secular or clerical calling is yours, Holy Spirit is there creating and moving through your sphere of influence. The Kingdom of God is not about better church meetings. Holy Spirit wants to work individually through you to release the substance of the Kingdom throughout society. He is an artist, longing to paint His love through the medium of your life.

But it would be a grave mistake to believe Holy Spirit is merely a means to some greater end. He is not simply a force that makes you more productive. Not just a mechanical power that helps you to win more souls or build a bigger ministry.

There is no other end except for Him. He is not just an enabler. He is the very Goal Itself. God is not looking for a performance oriented "purpose-driven" church. God is looking for an *intimacy-driven* church. A Spirit-driven, Glory-driven church that is compelled by love for Him. As a matter of fact, God is the One driving His church, and we are being chauffeured by grace! God is not looking for moral people who do good works on His assembly line. He does not need workers; He wants bridal lovers. There is no other purpose than His Glory. If there is work to be done, then the lovers will outwork the workers.

Since Holy Spirit is a *spirit being*, we should understand that He has a personality and traits. He speaks (Tim. 4:1); He has a will (1 Cor. 12:11); He is knowledgeable (1 Cor. 2:11), He teaches (John 14:26); He has a mind (Rom. 8:27); He loves (Rom. 15:30); and He can also be grieved or insulted (Eph. 4:30; Heb. 10:29).

Furthermore, He is eternal, omnipresent – *existing everywhere* – and He is omniscient – *knows everything* (1 Cor. 2:10, 11; Ps. 139:7-10). Scripture is clear that He was involved in the creation of the world, along with the Father and the Son. He brought life to mankind as He was exhaled by the Father.

Holy Spirit is personally involved and necessary for the salvation of every soul. No one would ever be able to meet or receive Jesus unless Holy Spirit drew them. He convicts the world of sin. He works miracles. He reveals the will of God. He continually points us to Jesus. Holy Spirit confirms that Jesus is the Christ (Acts 2:22), and He continually aided Jesus to confirm His work (Matt. 12:28; Luke 4:18-21). The only interaction you have *ever* had with God has been through the agency of Holy Spirit.

Holy Spirit is not somehow relegated to the third and lowest rung on the ladder of the Trinity. He is not somehow less than the Father or the Son. He is equally God. He is due worship and honor as God. He is clearly a distinct member of the Trinity. He is not to be ignored. Some denominations would prefer to believe in the Father, Son and Holy Bible. Their concept of an interpersonal relationship with God the Spirit *in the now* has either been truncated by poor theology, lack of experience or fear of the unknown.

Holy Spirit does not want to be ignored. He wants to be *enjoyed.*

INTRODUCTION

Holy Spirit is closer than the air you breathe. There is no need to chase or pursue Him. If He is in you, and you are in Him, then why are you still looking for Him? If you are a believer, He lives inside of you, "*because you are sons, God sent the Spirit of His Son into our hearts*" (Gal. 4:6, NIV).

And the Spirit of the Lord shall rest upon Him,
The Spirit of Wisdom and Understanding,
The Spirit of Counsel and Might,
The Spirit of Knowledge
and of the Fear of the Lord

\+ ISAIAH 11:1-2

+ CHAPTER ONE
THE LAMPSTAND

One of the most cryptic references in the Book of Revelation is to the seven Spirits of God burning before the throne in Heaven. For ages, the seven Spirits have eluded scholars and sparked wonder in the hearts of believers, hungry to peer into the mysterious depths of the invisible realm.

We are living in a day when the Lord is revealing hidden truths and restoring ancient pathways. He has stripped the veils of Heaven, and He has granted us access to His inner sanctuary. For those who are hungry, whose cry is "Oh, that You would rend the heavens! That You would come down," their prayer has been answered in the giving of His Son.[2]

The heavens are already open. The blood of Christ is a powerful solvent, breaking through every religious veneer, through every shroud and through every enigma that holds us back from understanding Him more. Truly the riddle of the sevenfold Spirit of God is a mystery, or *mysterion,* as St. John the Revelator tells us. Something that does not come easily to the understanding through casual observation – yet the Spirit who reveals all truth to us, invites us to explore the nature and personality of God by His free gift of grace.

In the following chapters, our goal is to travel far beyond those veils and to apprehend the deep dynamics of the sevenfold nature of Holy Spirit. Today, the Lord is speaking more about this subject in the Body of Christ than perhaps ever before in history. The Lord is reveal-

---

[2] See Isa. 64:1

ing His seven Spirits not just for the purpose of intellectual curiosity. Nor is this revelation simply a matter of cognitive *talk*, but the Lord is releasing explosive demonstrations of *power* through His servants.[3] As you are established in the truth about God's sevenfold nature, the person of Christ should be more brilliantly reflected to you. And a greater manifestation of the Spirit's virtue, favor, ability and intimate interactions should manifest in your life. The sevenfold virtue of Holy Spirit speaks of His fullness flowing through the life of the believer.

Our call is to enjoy participation as God brings Heaven to Earth *through us*. We birth substance from the invisible realm into the visible world around us. The church, like Mary, is a womb that is called to give birth to a tangible expression of Christ in the Earth. Our goal is not merely to learn about the nature of the Spirit, but to be fully possessed and inundated by Him. Under the loving shade of His presence, we both conceive the Word, and we labor give birth to it.[4] The job description of a true believer is not to simply be a hearer of the word only, but a *doer* of the word.[5] That means our lives are to manifest physical signposts of unseen, heavenly realities.

God is raising up a generation to meet this task. A church that will both understand and appropriate the mysteries of Heaven. This is a body of people who will comprehend the hidden things of His Kingdom, and they will also demonstrate His power for the world to

---

[3] See 1 Cor. 4:20

[4] Song of Sol. 8:5

[5] See Jas. 1:22

take notice. This is a company of believers on the rise who will literally shine forth the *fullness* of God. Our study of the sevenfold Spirit is an *unpackaging* of this fullness, which has already taken hold of us!

What does the fullness of God look like, and how do we take hold of it? Jesus Christ has all the fullness of the Godhead dwelling in His flesh. And through the finished work of the cross, He says that you have *already received it as a gift*!

> *For in Christ the Godhead in all its fullness dwells incarnate and, by your union with Him, you also are filled with it. ...* [6]

What does this verse mean? It means you have *all of God* living in your belly! If a person began to believe and manifest just one percent of this truth, it would be enough to turn the world upside down. You not only have Jesus inside of you. Not only Holy Spirit. You also have the Father inside of you … He who breathed the universe into existence. Thomas Aquinas wrote, "The whole Trinity dwells in the mind by sanctifying grace, according to John 14:23: 'We will come to him, and will make Our abode with him.'"[7]

Again, John says, "*of His fullness we have all received, and grace upon grace.*"[8]

The Christian sojourn is simply a process of discovering the gift of God we have already received. We are

---

[6] Col. 2:9-10, TCNT

[7] Thomas Aquinas, *Summa Theologica*, First Part Q. 43, Article 5.

[8] John 1:16, NASB

merely being established in our faith – to deepen our belief and comprehension of what the finished work of the cross has already purchased for us, in us and through us. The Lord wants us to experience this complete fullness. He has given us rich, unbroken communion with His presence just as Adam had in the garden of pleasure. The purpose for fresh revelation is simply to awaken us to believe the truth at a deeper level, so that we can experience it and ultimately enjoy Him more. God wants us to fully know Him, even as we are fully known.[9] His goal is to have our hearts consumed with His holy fire.

+ THE SEVENFOLD NATURE OF THE SPIRIT

The sevenfold nature of the Spirit has been a sorely neglected subject, largely because theologians did not know what to do with it. It sounds far too polytheistic to suggest that there are *seven* Spirits instead of one. And this is the same sort of stumbling block that posed difficulty for the Jews in accepting the deity of Christ. The seeming plurality of the Trinity is a mystery that could not be fathomed by the monotheistic Hebrews, who knew that "the Lord is God; besides Him there is no other."[10]

> *Hear, O Israel: The Lord our God, the Lord is one.*[11]

He is one, indeed. But this One is also *threefold*. He is Father, Son and Holy Spirit. This concept of a three-in-

---

9 See 1 Cor. 13:12
10 See Deut. 4:35
11 See Deut. 6:4

one God was problematic for the Pharisee. But it was also problematic for the *prophets*. In the seventh chapter of Daniel, the writer was severely troubled because his monotheistic Jewish paradigm was being challenged. He knew of the Ancient of Days. But then Daniel had a vision of one like a *son of man* coming and receiving everlasting dominion from the Ancient of Days.

"I, Daniel, was grieved in my spirit within my body," he writes, "and the visions of my head troubled me."[12] He was getting a glimpse of the Trinity, of God's three-in-one nature, and it overwhelmed him. The revelation was too much for his theological framework. In a similar way, Holy Spirit is one, yet He is also *sevenfold.* Time eternal will not exhaust the enigma of the Trinity. We can learn much about the roles and interaction of the Father, Son and Spirit, but much more remains unexplained. Much is unknown, yet somehow *all* is revealed in Christ. Though we will cover much ground, we should not expect to completely grasp the Spirit's sevenfold nature from just one book. In fact, the things of the Spirit are *supernaturally* discerned. They do not come merely from books. They require personal interaction and relationship with Him.

> *This is what we speak, not in words taught us by human wisdom but in words taught by the Spirit, expressing spiritual truths in spiritual words. The man without the Spirit does not accept the things that come from the Spirit of God, for they are fool-*

---

[12] Dan. 7:15, NKJV

> *ishness to him, and he cannot understand them, because they are spiritually discerned.*[13]

It is Holy Spirit who must enlighten us. Beyond our mental capabilities, to comprehend the depth of His nature. Even the reading of scripture alone will not do this for us. The Spirit must illuminate the written word if we are to grasp its meaning and intent. The Spirit brings the word *alive*. In fact, He is the *Spirit of Life*. And life, like love, is not easily defined. It is just lived. It is not taught, as much as it is caught. God's Spirit is His very essence. To say He is sevenfold is not to say He is seven *separate persons*. However, one could say there are seven elements, dynamics or characteristics of the same Spirit. Moreover, there are seven *operations* or flows of the same Spirit. These are what we will explore.

"He is called the seven spirits, not with regard to His essence, which is one, but with regard to His manifold operations," writes John Wesley.[14]

The seven Spirits of God are mentioned four times in the Book of Revelation. The Apostle John first mentions the seven Spirits while addressing the seven churches in Asia, then refers to them three more times:

> *John,*
> *To the seven churches in the province of Asia: Grace and peace to you from Him who is, and who was, and who is to come, and from the* ***seven spirits***

---

[13] 1 Cor. 2:13-14, NIV

[14] John Wesley, *John Wesley's Notes on the Whole Bible: The New Testament* (Available online at www.ccel.org), Notes on The Revelation of John.

before His throne, and from Jesus Christ, who is the faithful witness, the firstborn from the dead, and the ruler of the kings of the Earth.[15]

To the angel of the church in Sardis write: These are the words of Him who holds the ***seven spirits of God*** *and the seven stars. ...*[16]

From the throne came flashes of lightning, rumblings and peals of thunder. Before the throne, seven lamps were blazing. These are the ***seven Spirits of God****.*[17]

Then I saw a Lamb, looking as if it had been slain, standing in the center of the throne, encircled by the four living creatures and the elders. He had seven horns and seven eyes, which are the ***seven spirits of God*** *sent out into all the Earth.*[18]

The "seven Spirits" are the "seven eyes" of God. They are the "seven lamps of fire." Because there has been little revelatory teaching on this subject, it is important to lay some strong Biblical foundations. Over the course of this volume, we will see these seven echoed throughout the scripture, from the very beginning.

We should note that the word "seven" here is *hepta* in the Greek, which is also used elsewhere in scripture to

---

[15] Rev. 1:4-5, NIV

[16] Rev. 3:1, NIV

[17] Rev. 4:5, NIV

[18] Rev. 5:6, NIV

mean "sevenfold."[19] It is the word translated from the Hebrew, for example, when Cain was banished from the land in Genesis 4. The Lord said that if anyone killed Cain, that person would suffer "sevenfold" or "seven times over."[20] The context of "hepta" can determine whether it means seven *separate* objects or one single *sevenfold* object. It is interchangeable.

The New Living Translation renders the text as "the sevenfold Spirit before His throne."[21]

The word "spirits," or *pneumata/pneumaton,* is plural in structure.[22] But this does not prevent it from being a single object that is plural in nature. For instance, the Hebrew name for God, *Elohim*, is a plural word, which is contextually used to refer to One God. However, we know that it speaks of a three-in-one Trinity.

More important than splitting hairs over Greek words, it is vital that we have a basic understanding of the spirit realm and different heavenly beings, which we will discuss in later chapters. Because there are commentators who suggest that the seven Spirits of God are angels, pastors, extraneous spirit beings, etc., it is vital that we learn to navigate the spirit realm a bit. Not subjectively, but scripturally. We should understand the difference between God's Spirit, our personal human spirits, angels, demons, creatures and spiritual virtues. This will

---

[19] James Strong, *Exhaustive Concordance of the Bible* (Nashville: Abingdon, 1890), Entry 2033.

[20] See Gen 4:15

[21] Rev. 1:4, NLT

[22] Strong, *Exhaustive Concordance of the Bible*, Entry 4151.

not only deepen our understanding of God's sevenfold nature, but will also guard us from deception.

Since we may be correcting some existing pop doctrines and theological error in the Body of Christ, I should note that there is only one way to interpret the Bible. *We interpret scripture with scripture.* The Word of God interprets itself. We do not rely solely on experience, denominational preference or tradition. Nor do we base our doctrines on revelatory experiences we have had. God does use subjective experiences to heighten our quest for truth and to reveal the Word. But the Word is Truth.

Holy Spirit is One, only sevenfold in *personality*. Many have misconstrued the sevenfold Spirit of God to mean that there are seven gods. In fact, the Book of Revelation because of its cryptic language has been the fodder for numerous cults. An even more widespread error, especially in the charismatic church today, is to think that these are seven angels. This is also a major deception, though an understandable one due to the mystique of the passage. The error is due largely to the mention of the *seven angels* of the seven churches that are alongside the seven Spirits of God in these scriptures. We will discuss this briefly.

+ The Seven Angels & Seven Spirits

From the onset in the Book of Revelation, we are greeted in the name of the Trinity. We see that the churches are offered grace and peace *on behalf* of the seven Spirits in Revelation 1:4-5. Again, read this initial benediction from the entire Trinity:

> *... from Him who is, and who was, and who is to come, and from the seven spirits before His throne, and from Jesus Christ.*[23]

Clearly the Father is "Him who is, and who was, and who is to come." Scholars overwhelmingly agree that John bends grammatical rules in this line, just so that he can conform the Greek syntax to reflect Father God's name as the Hebrew "I am" of Exodus 3:14.

Jesus Christ the Son is directly named as well. The question is why would seven angels be sandwiched between the Father and the Son in this benediction, while excluding Holy Spirit?

"The *seven Spirits* might conceivably refer to a group of angelic beings. But coming between references to the Father and the Son it is more probable that this is an unusual way of designating the Holy Spirit," notes New Testament commentator Rev. Canon Leon Morris.[24]

Perhaps the text simply means what it says. These are not the seven spirits of angels. Not the seven spirits of beings. They are the seven *Spirits of God*. This is not a new concept, nor a heretical notion. Theologians through the ages have come to the same conclusion. Translator William Barclay notes that Beatus of Liébana (c. 730-800) writes, "The Spirit is one in name but sevenfold in virtues." While Barclay himself adds, "Some think that (angels) are the seven Spirits men-

---

[23] Rev. 1:4-5, NIV

[24] Rev. Canon Leon Morris, *The Revelation of St. John: An Introduction and Commentary* (Grand Rapids: William B. Eerdmans Publishing Co., 1973), 48.

tioned here. But that cannot be; great as the angels were, they were still created beings."[25]

It is clear that early protestants knew the sevenfold to be the Spirit of God Himself, as indicated by marginal notes in the 1560 Geneva Bible – the first English version translated from the original languages. The commentary states that the seven Spirits are "signifying the fulnes of the Spirit, which Chriſt powreth vpon all (sic)."[26]

Furthermore, the prophet Isaiah tells us that this same sevenfold Spirit rested upon Jesus.[27] I promise you that Jesus was not anointed with angels. *The Spirit the Sovereign Lord* was upon Him.[28] Luke chapter four clarifies that Jesus was anointed with "The Spirit of the Lord." And we also know that Jesus had the Spirit *without measure*:

> *For the one whom God sent speaks the authentic words of God – and there can be no measuring of the Spirit given to Him!*[29]

Jesus has given us this same limitless supply of the Spirit of God through our union with Him. Your body is now a temple of His same Holy Spirit (1 Cor. 3:16). That Spirit lives within you, and now you too have Him *without measure*! You do not have a mini-sized God

---

[25] Barclay, *The Daily Study Bible Series: The Revelation of John, Vol. 1,* 31.

[26] *The Geneva Bible*, 1560 edition (Peabody, MA: Hendrickson Publishers, Inc., 2007 reprint).

[27] See Isa. 11:1-2

[28] See Isa. 61:1

[29] John 3:34, PHI

inside of you. You do not just have a portion of Him. You do not possess a *measurable* amount of God. If you are a son of God, then you have *the same Spirit that raised Jesus Christ from the dead* dwelling fully and completely inside of you.

> *... and you have been given fullness in Christ, who is the head over every power and authority.*[30]

This was made possible, because Christ possessed God in His entirety within His own human body.

> *For in Him the complete being of God, by God's own choice, came to dwell.*[31]

We will discuss this concept of *fullness* throughout these chapters, for this is really what the seven Spirits represent: a complete, perfect and total abundance of God in the substance of His Spirit in the life of the church. The number *seven*, throughout scripture represents completeness, wholeness or perfection.

It is sufficient for now that we begin merely to clarify the difference between Holy Spirit and the angels. It is for important reasons that the angels are listed alongside the seven Spirits in these passages. For there are angelic beings assigned to the ministry of these seven Spirits of God. The scriptures tell us angels "do the word" of God,[32] and that they are sent to serve those who inherit salvation.[33] It should therefore be no sur-

---

[30] Col. 2:10, NIV

[31] Col. 1:19, NEB

[32] See Ps. 103:20

[33] See Heb. 1:14

prise that angels are ministers or "releasers" of these seven facets of God's presence, but they are not the sevenfold Spirit of God Himself.

There is a pop doctrine floating about these days that the seven Spirits are a special order of beings or ethereal *tutors* that are sent to mature the sons of God. This started with one or two prophetic guys who claimed they had been personally mentored by these beings, therefore making them more mature than everyone else! They adamantly claim that the seven Spirits are not God Himself. Some would go so far as to say you are being religious if you disagree with them on this point.

We should always embrace angelic assistance, no doubt. Yet we can never base our theology on visions, experiences or inspired imaginations. If our doctrine doesn't come from the scriptures – just the slightest few degrees of error in our navigation can lead us to an entirely different destination.

There are two things at work here that we should understand. Angels are mouthpieces for God. But we are not mouthpieces for angels. In Revelation 1, John serves as a mouthpiece or *witness* for the Spirits of God, just as he also speaks for the Father (who is, and who was, and who is to come) and for the Son (Jesus Christ, who is the faithful witness). Since John is speaking on behalf of the Father and the Son, it would only make sense that the "seven Spirits" refer to Holy Spirit, in whose name he also sends greetings. It would be odd, even unprecedented, for John to testify for angels – who themselves are messengers. The word "angel" means *messenger*.

In addition, John extends "grace and peace" from these persons, and we know that angels are not the ultimate source of grace or peace. God is the source, though angels can be pass-through vessels of such virtues.

Another important key is found in Revelation 3:1 where John makes a distinction between the seven Spirits and the seven stars. He separates them, saying "*These are the words of Him who holds the seven Spirits* ***and*** *the seven stars.*"

The Spirits and the stars are different.

We know from Revelation 1:20 what these seven stars are – *they are angels*:

> *The mystery of the seven stars that you saw in my right hand and of the seven golden lampstands is this: The* ***seven stars are the angels*** *of the seven churches, and the seven lampstands are the seven churches.*[34]

John makes a clear distinction between the Spirits of God and His angelic servants. One could do an extensive study on the seven angels, comparing them to the attributes of the seven Asian churches. But we don't have time for that now. It is sufficient to know that angels are "ministering spirits," while the sevenfold Spirit of God is far beyond comparison with angelic majesties or any other spiritual beings.

John Wesley notes that the seven Spirits are never found to be worshipping:

---

[34] Rev. 1:20, NIV

> *By these seven spirits, not seven created angels, but the Holy Ghost is to be understood. The angels are never termed spirits in this book; and when all the angels stand up, while the four living creatures and the four and twenty elders worship Him that sitteth on the throne, and the Lamb and the seven spirits neither stand up nor worship. To these "seven spirits of God," the seven churches, to whom the Spirit speaks so many things, are subordinate; as are also their angels, yea, and "the seven angels which stand before God."*[35]

Finally, we should address one more line of reasoning from those who would insist that these are angels. Some would point out that since these Spirits are *before the throne*, it implies that they are not God – as God Himself would logically be seated on the throne.

We must remember that Holy Spirit is *not on the throne*. Or perhaps more correctly I should say He is not *only* on the throne. Holy Spirit is *God in the Earth.* It is via Holy Spirit in the Earth that the Father has His omniscience (all seeing, all knowing) and omnipresence (the Presence of God everywhere). "He is before the throne; for, as God made, so He governs, all things by His Spirit," writes commentator Matthew Henry.[36]

---

[35] John Wesley, *John Wesley's Notes on the Whole Bible: The New Testament* (Available online at www.ccel.org), Notes on The Revelation of John.

[36] Matthew Henry, *Matthew Henry's Commentary on the Whole Bible* (Grand Rapids: Zondervan Publishing House, 1960), 1970.

Holy Spirit is *God everywhere*. And the reason He is pictured before the throne, shining on Jesus, is because He always points to Jesus and illuminates Him.

> *Where can I go from your Spirit? Where can I flee from your presence? If I go up to the heavens, you are there; if I make my bed in the depths, you are there. If I rise on the wings of the dawn, if I settle on the far side of the sea, even there your hand will guide me, your right hand will hold me fast.*[37]

The word "depths" is literally *sheol* (it is the pit, the dead or even in some translations *hell*). Holy Spirit is everywhere. He takes up all the space! He is unavoidable. Although hell is a real place, it is truly a man's own self-imposed prison – a make-believe world of pretending that God isn't there. Like Adam after he ate the fruit, a sinner is trying to hide from a God who is everywhere. God is omnipresent. Satan is a "less than nothing" because God is too big and occupies everything. Satan is a *minus*. This is why sin is such a delusion. There's not only *no existence* apart from God. The fallen state is a "less than" or negative existence. There is no place you can run apart from Him, because there is no room left over. And so, in one sense, hell is a psychotic non-existence of separation from a God who exists everywhere. C.S. Lewis writes:

> ... *every state of mind, left to itself, every shutting up of the creature within the dungeon of its own mind – is, in the end, Hell. But Heaven is not a state*

[37] Ps. 139:7-10, NIV

> *of mind. Heaven is reality itself. All that is fully real is Heavenly.*[38]

Lewis says the damned and the saint are in the same place – *reality* – but that the damned hate it. Hell grows up within like a disease that finally takes a man over. He has finally locked himself into an eternal state of rejecting goodness. As Dostoyevsky writes, "We are all in paradise, but we do not want to know it."[39]

Our goal in these pages is to have our eyes opened to the presence of God and awakened to the fullness of Him that is always in us and with us as believers.

+ Back to the Future

The Book of Revelation is chock full of dark sayings and parabolic language. Much of it has layers of meaning, both literal and allegorical. Most of it is intentionally shrouded (*for us*, not from us) with broad layers of fulfillment that is historical, present tense and futuristic. There are blessings for those who read and keep it – but no command that we must figure it out. It's a fun book to explore. It exhorts us and comforts us on a personal level. It reveals the nature of God, and it is His Word. But I never trust a man's eschatology that is too dogmatic on its interpretation. Apocalyptic works are not to be disregarded, but they must be read with the heart as much as with the cognitive mind. And we must be content to stay in the turbid waters of holy mysticism, for

---

[38] C.S. Lewis, *The Great Divorce* (New York: HarperCollins Publishers, 1946), 70.

[39] Fyodor Dostoevsky, *The Brothers Karamazov*, translated by Richard Pevear and Larissa Volokhonsky (New York: Farrar, Straus and Giroux, 1990), 288.

rigid assertions and unbending views choke its animation and blind us to its deeper rays.

This thesis on the sevenfold is by no means an *end-times* book. But this is a prophetic exploration that draws on words and imagery intended for the last days bride. Our study here is less of an interpretation of future events, as it is an application of present heavenly realities. The reality of God *with us*. While our understanding of seven horns, seven eyes, seven churches, seven stars and the many other strange and unusual typologies listed in the Book of Revelation may remain truncated, we will nevertheless gain a stronger paradigm for the movement of Holy Spirit in our present lives.

For now, we begin our journey by going backward in time several thousand years to recover a very basic blueprint: *the lampstand of the Tabernacle.*

+ The Church is the Lampstand

> *I turned around to see the voice that was speaking to me. And when I turned I saw seven golden lampstands, and among the lampstands was someone "like a son of man," dressed in a robe reaching down to His feet and with a golden sash around His chest.*[40]

John was "in a trance" or literally "spirit possessed" on the Lord's Day when he had an encounter with Jesus in the midst of seven golden lampstands. John turned to "see the voice." In His hand, Jesus was holding seven

---

[40] Rev. 1:12-13, NIV

stars. This picture of Christ among the lampstands was part of a *mystery* that the Lord goes on to interpret for us:

> *The mystery of the seven stars that you saw in my right hand and of the seven golden lampstands is this: The seven stars are the angels of the seven churches, and the* ***seven lampstands are the seven churches.***[41]

This is one clear and simple interpretation that opens up a world of understanding for us …

The churches are lampstands.

By comparing the church to the lampstand, Christ instantly interprets for us a plethora of Old Testament passages that speak directly into *your identity* as a believer. In this half sentence, in fact, Christ opens up chapter upon chapter of revelation on the nature of His Holy Spirit. The lampstand plays such an important role in the history of Judaism, that today it is still the national symbol. Little do they know, but the Jews are pointing to the *Christian church* as their state emblem! God still has powerful plans for natural Israel, but be assured that it will only be as they are grafted back into Him through Christ.

The lampstand was one of the original utensils used for worship in the Mosaic Tabernacle, constructed according to a pattern prescribed by God. The Old Covenant provided an earthly pattern of worship that we now know was only symbolic of "the greater and more per-

---

[41] Rev. 1:20, NIV

fect tabernacle that is not man-made."[42] That earthly tent was a blueprint of Christ – a shadow of the heavenly sanctuary of God's presence, opened up to us once and for all on the cross. All of the tables, altars, articles and instruments used in those days were symbolic of things to come, all reflecting a greater covenant that would one day be fulfilled in Christ.

The tabernacle was divided into three sections: the Outer Court, the Holy Place and the Most Holy Place. No one entered the Most Holy Place, except for the high priest who entered only once a year, and never without blood, which he offered both for his own sins and the sins of the people. A rope would be tied to his leg, because if he did not find favor with God, he would have to be dragged out dead. That room was blocked off from the people by a thick veil. In that Holy of Holies – what we may now deem the *Heaven of Heavens* – the only light was the light of the Lord. All believers are now seated in that Heaven of Heavens with Him and in Him,[43] and He is the only light that is needed there – not the light of the sun nor a lamp, but the Lord God, who is more brilliant than the sun.[44]

Get it out of your mind that Heaven is the place where Christ lives. It's not that Christ is in Heaven, but that Heavenly realms exist *within* Christ. The heavens can't contain Him.

---

42 Heb. 9:11, NIV

43 See Eph. 2:6

44 See Rev. 22:5

THE LAMPSTAND

And God raised us up with Christ and seated us with Him in the heavenly realms ***in Christ Jesus***.[45]

Christ Jesus is our High Priest, who gives us access into the Most Holy Place once and for all with His own blood. On one hand, we are already seated in this Holy of Holies – here in Heaven with Him. And yet, our natural bodies are still here on Earth. At all times, we have unbroken access to that spiritual realm. Our union with Christ in this place is not based on our feelings or emotions. We do not have access to the Holy of Holies because it *feels like it*. We have access because of His blood. We are in mystical union with Christ right here now and forever.

While we are spiritually seated there in Heaven, our bodies are nevertheless still walking on the ground. In a sense, Christians are in-between creatures. We are two places at once. In the holiest place, yet walking among the nations of this world. While we are here, our call is to reflect the light of Christ in the middle room. The middle room of the tabernacle was the *Holy Place*. That is where the lampstand was located. It was "in-between" the Holy of Holies and the Outer Courts.

To say we are *in-between* does not suggest that we aren't already perfected by His sacrifice – for we are spotless. These are only rudimentary images of a primitive religion – but they foreshadow, in striking detail, how the church is called to shine our light while still suspended between Heaven and Earth. The lampstand, you could say, is suspended between two realms of existence: the temporal and the eternal.

---

[45] Eph. 2:6, NIV

While the Holy of Holies shone with the shekinah Glory, the lampstand was able to give off *some* light. *Again, the lampstand represents the church.* We are shining with the illumination of God's Spirit, pointing the world to Christ. The lampstand always shone upon the table of shewbread. This was symbolic of the fact that we always point to the person of Christ, who is the Bread of Life.

The church has often been compared to the moon, having no light of its own. The moon reflects the light of the sun, just as we reflect the light of Christ. This is partially true. However, Christ dwells *within us*, therefore we are able to burn with His brilliance from the inside out. In this sense, we are more appropriately like the sun itself:

> *... the righteous will* ***shine like the sun*** *in the Kingdom of their Father.*[46]

> *Who is this that appears like the dawn, fair as the moon,* ***bright as the sun****, majestic as the stars in procession?*[47]

Jesus was the "*brightness of His Glory, and the express image*" of the invisible God.[48] He said that *if you see me, you have seen the Father.*[49] The church has this same mandate. When the world sees us, they should see the Lord. We are His ambassadors – His representatives

---

46 Matt. 13:43, NIV

47 Song of Sol. 6:10, NIV

48 See Heb. 1:3

49 See John 14:9

– His hands and feet in this world. In Christ, we are a *chosen people, a royal priesthood.*[50] We are all doing priestly duties and representing Him, just as Christ, our High Priest, represented the Father.

We are blazing lampstands, shining with the light of His grace. It is His light that burns within us, and it is upon Him that we shine and illuminate His Glory.

+ Blueprints of the Menorah

Understanding the blueprints of the Old Testament lampstand is an important key to understanding the seven Spirits of God that flow through the life of the church. Everyone is familiar with the traditional *menorah* that has come to represent the Jewish holiday of Hanukkah. The word "menorah" is Hebrew for *lampstand* or *candlestick.* It is the same word used by God when giving instructions for its construction it in Exodus 25 and repeated verbatim in Exodus 37:

> *Make a lampstand of pure gold and hammer it out, base and shaft; its flowerlike cups, buds and blossoms shall be of one piece with it. Six branches are to extend from the sides of the lampstand – three on one side and three on the other. Three cups shaped like almond flowers with buds and blossoms are to be on one branch, three on the next branch, and the same for all six branches extending from the lampstand. And on the lampstand there are to be four cups shaped like almond flowers with buds and blossoms. One bud shall be under the first pair of branches extending from the lampstand, a second*

50 See 1 Pet. 2:9

bud under the second pair, and a third bud under the third pair – six branches in all. The buds and branches shall all be of one piece with the lampstand, hammered out of pure gold.

Then make its seven lamps and set them up on it so that they light the space in front of it. Its wick trimmers and trays are to be of pure gold. A talent of pure gold is to be used for the lampstand and all these accessories. See that you make them according to the pattern shown you on the mountain.[51]

The lampstand in the Old Testament was just that: a *stand* that was designed to hold seven separate lamps on the top of it. The churches are no more than *stands* – or carriers – but the actual light is Christ, whom we show forth. The seven flaming lamps – which rest on top of the stand – are the seven Spirits of God that burn continually on it. Again, picture the modern day menorah still used today during Hanukah.

Just as candles are placed on top of the lampstand at Hanukah, in the same way, the priests were to place seven lamps on the top of the seven-branched stand. Revelation 4:5 tells us what these actual lamps were:

Before the throne, seven lamps (not the stand) *were blazing. These are the seven spirits of God.*

The lampstand (church) that holds these lamps (seven Spirits) is made of one single piece of pure gold. This symbolizes the unity and purity needed for a church that would hold the fullness of the sevenfold Spirit. No-

---

[51] Exod. 25:31-40, NIV

tice that God did not use three hundred denominations of gold. Rather, He has built His church of *one piece* of gold – gold representing His own deity. All who are believers, regardless of denomination, worship style or local church affiliation – we are all the mystical Body of Christ.

There is much prophetic insight to be gained from the very shape of the lampstand. Here, in the divine model, we have the seven branches laid out in an orderly pattern. This seven-branched lampstand consists of one central shaft, out of which flow six others. The church is the Lord's body. The central shaft represents the presence of the Lord within the believer, and flowing outward from the center branch are the six others. This represents the Spirit flowing out through mankind. Six is the number of man. Man is only complete when the Lord is at His center, making the seven of completion.

These six branches came out of the sides of the lampstand, even as the water and blood flowed from the Lord's side. In the same way, He is the vine, and we are the branches – His Spirit is the sap or nutrient that flows through us to bear fruit.

+ The Almond Tree

As you noticed in the blueprint given by God for construction of the menorah, it is to be ornately constructed with a specific number of almond flowers, buds and blossoms on each branch. Every detail here has prophetic significance. In Israel, the almond tree is the first tree to blossom in the springtime. The word for almond tree literally means *watching* or *waking*. It is the first tree to *wake up* from the winter. The seven Spirits of

God, or the *eyes of the Lord*, are couched in an awakened church, whose eyes and hearts are opened to the things of the Spirit.

This should bring understanding to the following verse in Jeremiah 1:11-12:

> *The word of the Lord came to me: "What do you* ***see****, Jeremiah?" "I* ***see*** *the* ***branch of an almond tree****," I replied. The Lord said to me, "You have* ***seen*** *correctly, for I am* ***watching*** *to see that my word is fulfilled."*[52]

Notice how much Jeremiah "sees" when referring to the almond tree. This watching and awakening symbolism also points to the resurrection power foretold in the staff of Aaron, which supernaturally sprouted, budded, blossomed and produced almonds. In Numbers 17:1-12, we read of this account. Aaron's rod, which represented the priestly house of Levi, was one of the items placed inside the Ark of the Covenant. It represented the resurrection power of the cross – the authority given to the priesthood of believers.

When we count up all of the various almond parts on the lampstand – flowers, buds, blossoms, etc. – we find a total of *sixty-six parts*. Did you know that there are sixty-six books in your Bible? This is an ancient confirmation of the canon of scripture. These sixty-six almond parts are melded into the lampstand and are one piece with it. In the same way, the word of God is melded into us, the church. We are living epistles, in

[52] Jer. 1:11-12, NIV

complete union with the Word of God that is fused into our very DNA.

Never let anyone try to convince you that religious leaders suppressed other books of the Bible, or that apocryphal works hold the same weight of authority as the canon of scripture. Some apocryphal works are helpful, but they are not infallible. We never base theology on apocryphal works; they only serve to support the Word.

The seven lamps sat atop seven branches, each with three fruit, three flowers and three buds. There were nine ornaments in all – which are likewise symbolic of the nine fruits of Holy Spirit. All had their source in three originating buds, *the Trinity*. Keep in mind that the fruits of the Spirit are *Spirit-produced!* They are not the fruits of your own self.

Likewise the almond plant is seen in three stages – budding, flowering and fruitfulness. This is indicative of the tree itself waking up. *Watching* and *waking up* are synonymous terms here. On top of the menorah, the lamps of oil rested on the fully formed fruit of the waking tree – the watching tree. A living tree of life.

Jesus in the gospels commends us to "watch and pray." It is one thing to pray. It is another thing to have revelatory understanding. To see Him and be aware of the person of Christ. Likewise, we dwell in the seer realm, watching with the eyes of the heart to continually see what Heaven is doing.

The prophetic imagery of the lampstand is full of watching and seeing. The seven Spirits of God are the *seven eyes of the Lord, which range throughout the Earth.*[53]

The prophet Zechariah had a "wakening" experience with the lampstand of God. Unlike the lampstand in the Mosaic tabernacle of old, Zechariah saw some powerful prophetic modifications that we will discuss in the next section. Zechariah's experience began with these words:

> *Now the angel who talked with me came back and* ***wakened me****, as a man who is* ***wakened out of his sleep****. And he said to me, "What do you* ***see****?"*
>
> *So I said, "****I am looking****, and there is a lampstand of solid gold with a bowl on top of it, and on the stand seven lamps with seven pipes to the seven lamps.*[54]

---

[53] See Zech. 4:10

[54] Zech. 4:1-2, NKJV

+ CHAPTER TWO
ZECHARIAH'S VISION

There is a constant supply of Holy Spirit's oil surging through the life of the believer. It does not come by means of prayer and fasting. It does not come by means of human effort, theological ascension, better church meetings, powerful speakers or lengthy tarrying. The gift of Holy Spirit is yours without measure because Christ was nailed to a tree.

Christ means "Anointed One" or literally, the *Smeared One*. He was smeared with the oil of God, having the Spirit without measure in limitless supply. When He died on the cross, a mystical transaction took place. *You died with Him*. You are now a new creation. Not simply a remade version of the old Adamic you. You are altogether new in quality, new in ability and even *new in kind*. You are something the world has yet to see – a new breed.

> *I consider myself as having died and now enjoying a second existence, which is simply Jesus using my body.*[55]

You have so much of God inside of you, thanks to the work of the cross, that you can literally *do anything*! Nothing is impossible for you, as we read *all things are possible for him who believes*.[56] The very enabling work of Holy Spirit inside of you is stronger than any nuclear force, more intelligent than the most complex computer technology, more personal than a mother's kiss. You have the same Spirit that raised Christ from

---

[55] Gal. 2:20, DIS

[56] See Mark 9:23

the dead inside the core of your personality.[57] The only condition that is merited from us to manifest this realm of fullness is to *believe.*

> *Most assuredly, I say to you, he who believes in Me, the works that I do he will do also; and greater works than these he will do, because I go to My Father.*[58]

Even this ability to believe comes as a gift of grace.

Jesus raised the dead, walked on water, levitated, healed the sick, multiplied food, created money, walked through walls and exercised authority over the winds and waves. How can we do greater works than Jesus? Because we have the same Spirit of Jesus living inside of us. In this "greater works" passage, Jesus was speaking of the Promise of the Father, which is Holy Spirit coming to dwell within us. He follows that statement with this explanation:

> *And I will pray the Father, and He will give you another Helper, that He may abide with you forever— the Spirit of truth, whom the world cannot receive, because it neither sees Him nor knows Him; but you know Him, for He dwells with you and will be in you. I will not leave you orphans; I will come to you.*[59]

---

[57] See Rom. 8:11

[58] John 14:12, NKJV

[59] John 14:16-18, NKJV

We are not orphans, because we are literally the seed or "sperma" of God![60] You have the DNA of God's spiritual seed – His Word – inside of your being. You are most literally a child, or offspring of the living God! You are not simply full of God in the way a jar is full of water. As His seed, you are infused with His very essence. You are yoked together with Him in the core nature of your being. His yoke is the yoke of mystical union.

You do not *earn* your Father's DNA. You do not "press in" for it. It's just who you are. There is nothing you do to gain Holy Spirit. Christianity is not a lifelong course of moral activities and performance. It is a whole new existence in God. You've been brought into a whole new world – a whole new paradigm of reality. It is not about *doing* but *being*.

+ Golden Pipes of Oil

It is now that we will turn to the vivid imagery of the prophet Zechariah who surely looked into our day – in both type and shadow. Zechariah, like Moses, saw the lampstand of the coming church, but his vision was very different from the pattern given on the mountain.

In the old pattern of Moses, the lamps of fire rested *on top* of the stand. This represented a portion of Holy Spirit enablement resting *upon* the priests and prophets of old. But Zechariah saw a unique lampstand.

Zechariah saw a lampstand with *seven channels* flowing through to its oil lamps, giving a constant supply of

---

[60] See 1 John 3:9

oil that never runs out! He saw two olive trees, which produce the olive oil. These trees dripped into a bowl-like receptacle that poured down into the pipes.

These golden pipes were continually feeding the oil lamps with a fresh supply of inexhaustible oil.

> *Now the angel who talked with me came back and wakened me, as a man who is wakened out of his sleep. And he said to me, "What do you see?"*
>
> *So I said, "I am looking, and there is a lampstand of solid gold with a bowl on top of it, and on the stand seven lamps with seven pipes to the seven lamps.*
>
> *"Two olive trees are by it, one at the right of the bowl and the other at its left." So I answered and spoke to the angel who talked with me, saying, "What are these, my lord?" Then the angel who talked with me answered and said to me, "Do you not know what these are?"*[61]

After giving a relevant prophecy about Zerubbabel, governor of Judah (whom we will later discuss), the angel more specifically explains the vision of the lampstand and the two olive trees.

> *"For these seven rejoice to see the plumb line in the hand of Zerubbabel. They are the eyes of the Lord, which scan to and fro throughout the whole Earth."*
>
> *Then I answered and said to him, "What are these*

---

61 Zech. 4:1-5, NKJV

two olive trees—at the right of the lampstand and at its left?" And I further answered and said to him, "What are these two olive branches that drip into the receptacles of the two gold pipes from which the golden oil drains?"

Then he answered me and said, "Do you not know what these are?" And I said, "No, my lord." So he said, "These are the two anointed ones, who stand beside the Lord of the whole Earth."[62]

Before we attempt to interpret these passages, it is possible to begin applying them to our lives. The two olive trees feed the bowl, and the bowl feeds the lamps. The bowl is a reservoir of oil that is collected and funneled through the pipes into the flames of the seven lamps.

This revelation of Holy Spirit – as the seven lamps of fire blazing before the throne – is the same Holy Spirit that burns in the life of the church and the individual believer. He is the constant supply of abundant oil pouring from within your inner man. He enables you to burn with His incandescent flame of His seven Spirits, or His seven eyes. Inwardly we are drawing from His spiritual life source, like the lampstand draws from its never-ending supply of oil.

The believer does not simply possess a singular lamp, as some would surmise from scripture. Luke 12:35 says you have *multiple* lamps, "Let your waist be girded and your lamps burning." The lamps of God are resting on you, but His oil is also flowing up through you.

---

[62] Zech. 4:10:14, NKJV

In the older tabernacle, the lamps of fire rested *on top* of the almond cups. Picture for a moment, these small, handheld oil lamps – not unlike the portable lamps in the secular story of Aladdin, in which the genie dwells. These small lamps are what rested upon the stand in Moses' original blueprint. Each little oil lamp had a limited supply that required constant maintenance and continual refilling by the priests. These little lamps with their few ounces of oil represented just a little dab of Holy Spirit enablement resting upon the prophets of old. It required the constant work of an earthly priesthood. It represented a people who would be dabbled with oil on the *outside*. But when the oil burned up each day, they needed another refill.

But Zechariah sees a major difference here. In this new lampstand, we see the oil flowing constantly from the inside out. The pipes provide a steady stream. This represents the Spirit bubbling up from inside of you. Not from outside, but from interior union. The Spirit flows endlessly through the New Covenant church, because now God lives within the believer. We are not a people who get "filled up" then later require another refill. We are attached to the vine. There is constant influx. You are not a little paper cup that gets full, then emptied, filled again then dry. *There is no more room for dry seasons!* Instead, you are continually living under the waterfall. You have rivers flowing out of your inmost being. You are a channel, through which Holy Spirit constantly flows. Believers are open doors through which Heaven ceaselessly gushes in abundance. You have what the Latin Vulgate calls a "torrent of His pleasure" pouring from your inner man, enabling you to be *inebriated on the plenty of His house!*[63]

You are tapped into eternal reservoirs of this golden oil. With Christ in you, you are a source of oil on the Earth. With the Psalmist David, you can truly claim, "I am like an olive tree flourishing in the house of God."[64] The olive tree is a source of the oil. James Moffatt translates this passage of the Bible, calling the olive trees "*the sources of the oil of bliss*."[65]

There is no longer any lack in you. At the first moment of faith, Christ has caused you to become a *source* of blessing. Begin to believe it, and you will begin to manifest it. All of Heaven is within you and intends to pour through you. Luke 17:21 says the *Kingdom of God is within you.* You are much larger on the inside than the outside! From within you flow *multiple* rivers of Glory.

> *He who believes in Me, as the Scripture has said, out of his heart will flow rivers of living water.*[66]

Everywhere he goes, the life of the believer should spill and overflow with an abundance of the oil of favor. People should be blessed for receiving you; employers will be blessed by hiring you. Because of God's Glory on your life, everything you do can now prosper, because the Ark of His Presence rests in you, just as it once rested on the land of Obed Edom. Relationships

---

[63] Ps. 35:9, DRB

[64] Ps. 52:8, NIV

[65] Zech. 4:14, MOF

[66] John 7:38, NKJV

will be restored. The sick will be healed. The means and varieties of fruitfulness are endless. The Psalmist gives a beautiful picture of this. Scriptures literally tell us that the tracks of His chariot will drip with fatness! Not just the chariot, nor the chariot wheels. But even the tracks that you leave on the ground behind you will bubble up with riches, abundance and fatness because of the overflow of the favor and ability of Holy Spirit inside of you:

> *... where thy feet have passed, the stream of plenty flows.*[67]
>
> *You ... deluge your tracks with butterfat.*[68]
>
> *... your paths overflow with a rich harvest.*[69]
>
> *Thy footsteps are dropping with riches.*[70]

+ The Requirement is Faith

There is a sevenfold river of fullness existing within each believer's heart. The reason we do not always see this river fully *manifest*, is because there are not many believing believers! We are more prone to believe that Christ is one day going to do a work in us, than we are to believe that the work was finished from the foundation of the Earth.[71]

---

67 Ps. 65:11, KNOX
68 Ps. 65:11, ARTB
69 Ps. 65:11, NAB
70 Ps. 65:11, DEW
71 See Heb. 4:3

The Lord once showed me that most of His church today ascribes more to a quasi-Judaic leftover of Old Covenant theology than they do true New Testament Christianity. The good news is that Christ has opened all His treasuries and given you all your breakthroughs in one fell swoop on the cross! He has opened the House of Wine to you; He has opened the dimensions of His power; He has opened complete communion with Himself. In fact, He has held nothing back from you at all. On the cross, your old sinful nature was completely, once-and-for-all circumcised away,[72] and you were given access to a glorious new world. All of your problems really were solved on Golgotha's hill. It seems too good to be true. That's why it's called *good news*.

But in the charismatic movement today, of which I am considered a part, the yeast of Judaic religion still holds strong. For instance, people still pray and beg for holiness. They plead to be "purged." This alone is a telltale sign of absolute unbelief in the finished work of the cross. Religion wants you to kill yourself to earn holiness. There is a straining and a striving that is not suggestive of true faith. Jesus died to give you what you could never gain on your own. Religion gives us reams of books, keys and formulas for trying to get something that we already have as a *free gift*.

The problem is that most people are not *manifesting*, or outwardly showing forth the fullness of God. And so, they lower their theology to meet the standard of their experience, or lack thereof. They claim that holiness is

---

[72] See Col. 2

a result of a lifelong process of trials, asceticism, or whatever the latest trend tells them it requires.

As it turns out, the perfect sacrifice of Christ was actually good enough to get the job done. God happened to have this crazy notion one day that He could actually save the whole world single-handedly! If you are not manifesting a holy life, it is not because there is somehow more effort required on your part. If you are not manifesting a holy life, it is simply because *you do not believe*. This may sound harsh, but in truth, it is a relief. Stop striving for perfection, and rest in the fact that you have it. The nature and flavor of true faith is *rest.*[73] As I rest and trust that Christ has completed His work in me two thousand years ago, before I even got started – then I begin to act and live life like a completely different person. A person always manifests what he believes. If you believe you are holy, you will live holy. Believe you can heal the sick and you will. If the truth is your standard, the truth will experientially shine forth in your life. The Greek word for "truth" means *reality*. If you believe a lie – that you will always be wrestling with sin, or that you are a sinner – then guess what you will manifest?

Rest in the reality that Christ has fully changed you from one thing into another.

The gospel is a mystical message. You have to believe it before you see it. You must believe it before it bears tangible substance in your life.

---

[73] See See Heb. 4

Faith (belief) does have a tangible *substance* according to Hebrews 11:1. There is positive and negative faith – and depending what we expect, whether good or bad – that is the outcome we will receive. Rest assured that what you believe will surely be demonstrated in your life. True believing always involves *demonstration*. The Kingdom of Heaven is not a matter of mere talk, but of demonstration of power.[74]

Whatever you believe, you will demonstrate. If you think you are not yet capable or equipped enough to work miracles, you never will. If you believe that Christ's work was not enough, and somehow you need to help Him, then you will continue to struggle with sin, poverty, sickness and powerless living. But if you believe the *good news*, that Jesus took care of every single problem in the universe – then you're going to be quite the happy camper. You will begin to appropriate these riches. You will believe what the Bible actually says, that you *already have fullness in Him*. It's not a process. It's a gift.

We must have our minds renewed to believe the truth. The truth is that Christ has opened the Heavens already. He did away with our old Adamic nature. He has brought us into a glorious new existence in the family of God.

You have become an oasis in the desert. Your inner life bubbles up like pools of fresh water in a thirsty land. On one side of the cross, you were a beggar, longing or a blessing. But on this side of the cross, you have truly become a *source* of blessing. You are provision for the

---

[74] See 1 Cor. 4:20

hungry. You are drink for the thirsty. You are an endless supply of supernatural oil.

You forever flow with the golden oil of bliss!

+ THE INDWELLING SPIRIT

We have referenced the fact that, in the Old Covenant, the seven oil lamps were placed *on top* of the lampstand. In the same way, Holy Spirit generally rested *upon* His people in those days.

If a prophet of the Lord or a minister was raised up in the Old Testament, generally the scriptures say that the Spirit of the Lord *came upon* him. This was the case with figures such as Isaiah, Elijah and Elisha. Understand that this was a completely different concept from the New Covenant *indwelling* of the Holy Ghost. God does not come to rest upon us for an occasional visit. He has chosen to make His habitation within the sons of men. The first disciples asked Jesus, "Rabbi, where do You dwell?"[75] You are now a temple, in which He resides. The headwaters are within you, continually surging out of you. Like a radioactive substance, you are continually emitting the invisible rays of God into the world around you.

While there are a few isolated cases of the Lord "filling" someone or "entering into" someone, this continual abiding of God's presence was foreign to the Old Covenant, which was based on the rule and regulation of the law. The scriptures tell us that the fading Glory of the Old Covenant was so dismal in comparison with

---

[75] See John 1:38.

the ever-increasing Glory of this present one, that the New Covenant literally *eclipses* the former one, as the sun eclipses the moon.

The Old Covenant has no examples of anyone ever being filled with the *fullness* of God. The first example of someone being "full" of Holy Spirit was Jesus Himself in Luke 4:1. It is interesting to note that, in the few examples of Old Testament figures being "filled" with the Spirit, they were all direct representations of Christ or the church.

Filled, or *male'* in Hebrew, is used to describe only three Old Covenant people who were "filled with Holy Spirit."[76] One is the case of Joshua son of Nun (a prefigure type of Christ, whose very name *Yeshua* speaks for itself). Of course Joshua was not full of Holy Spirit in complete permanency, as believers are today. He was "filled with the Spirit of Wisdom" after Moses laid hands on him. But the scriptures never tell us was filled with the *fullness* of God's Spirit.

Interestingly, the only two others are Bezalel and Oholiab. These were the two artisans in charge of *building the lampstand!* Their lives were surely prophetic of the church being filled with God's Spirit. But again, their own "infilling" was restricted and qualified to a certain portion, related to their craft.

> *... and I have filled him with the Spirit of God,* ***with skill, ability and knowledge in all kinds of crafts***.[77]

---

[76] Strong, *Exhaustive Concordance of the Bible*, Entry 4390.

[77] Exod. 35:31, NIV

> *He has filled them* ***with skill to do all kinds of work as craftsmen. ...***[78]

The "filling" of Bezalel and Oholiab is primarily a prophetic shadow rather than an actualization of the New Covenant Spirit-filled life. Their names indicate that the Lord was moreover "upon" them, overshadowing them as a tent, rather than actually filling them as those with converted hearts. Bezalel means "in the shadow of God" and Oholiab means "my father's tent." I believe it is safe to say that they were filled with a portion or "unction" of the Spirit for a task, yet primarily God was still moving "upon" them. Nevertheless, the word *male'* is prophetic in its usage here.

At other times, the prophets were momentarily "entered" by God's Spirit.

> *And He said to me, "Son of man, stand on your feet, and I will speak to you." Then the Spirit entered me when He spoke to me, and set me on my feet; and I heard Him who spoke to me.*[79]

The Book of Micah tells us that the prophet was *male'* filled, not by the fullness of the Spirit, but by the *power* of God. This is the *Spirit of Might*, which is one of the sevenfold flows of the Spirit – something we will address in detail in a later chapter.

---

[78] Exod. 35:35, NIV

[79] Ezek. 2:1-2, NKJV

But truly I am full of power by the spirit of the Lord, and of judgment, and of might, to declare unto Jacob his transgression, and to Israel his sin.[80]

No one can argue that God moved in the lives of the prophets to a measured degree. The Book of Nehemiah has the following lament: *Yet for many years You had patience with them [Israel], And testified against them by Your Spirit* ***in Your prophets****. Yet they would not listen; Therefore You gave them into the hand of the peoples of the lands.*[81]

+ JOHN THE BAPTIST ... THE EXCEPTION?

The closest case of Holy Spirit "infilling" we see in the Old Covenant is the example of John the Baptist. The angel in the first chapter of Luke prophesied that John would be "filled" from birth. Likewise, both of his parents – Elizabeth and Zechariah – became filled. Although their lives are recorded in the Gospels, they were still under the Law. They were filled with the Spirit *prior* to the death and resurrection of Christ. Zechariah, "God Remembers," and Elizabeth, "God's Promise," came together to birth John, "Gods Gift of Grace." Truly Holy Spirit is the Promise of the Father, which He remembered in the giving of His own Son.

John's life was specifically indicative of the promised coming of Holy Spirit. Jesus stated he had come in the spirit of Elijah, and furthermore, that no person in history up to that point was greater than John the Baptist! What an incredible thing to say about an individual. But

[80] Mic. 3:8, KJV

[81] Neh. 9:30, NKJV

Jesus also said that the *least in the Kingdom of Heaven is greater than John.*[82]

The simplest believer in Christ is greater than John the Baptist. Why? Because through our faith in Christ, the Spirit comes to *permanently* dwell. And completely. By entering Christ, we have entered the Kingdom. Jesus was not talking about entering a future Heaven in the sky. He was talking about the least of all believers who are *in Him* are greater than the best of the best who were under the Law.

John did not have the Spirit permanently with Him, and even confessed his own worthlessness in comparison with Christ. This is why John spoke of Jesus saying:

> *I would not have known Him, except that the one who sent me to baptize with water told me, "The man on whom you see the Spirit come down* ***and remain*** *is He who will baptize with the Holy Spirit."*[83]

Jesus, not John, had Holy Spirit *permanently remaining* on Him. John recognized that he also needed to be baptized, telling Jesus, "You should be baptizing me!" John needed to be saved, just like everybody else.

John received his infilling from Jesus, when their mothers met and John was still in the womb. Somehow John recognized Jesus, even before he fully saw or understood the full manifestation. That is what made him great.

---

[82] See Matt. 11:11

[83] John 1:33, NIV

I do believe that John represents the gift of Holy Spirit to the believer. God remembers His Promise! What is the Promise of the Father? His Spirit of Grace that comes to dwell within the heart of the believer. Did you know that this is God's ultimate goal? The primary mandate of Jesus on the cross was not just to forgive you of sin. He did not come simply to take away something bad. He came to *fill you* with something good! The primary goal of redemption was not to empty you of evil, but rather to fill you with Himself. He could not fill sinful vessels, and so the work of the cross was necessary to eradicate the problem of sin. His ultimate purpose was to make you a temple of His Glory.

+ A Living Pneumatology

Our goal in this volume is to truly bring a revelation of the Spirit's operations. What is Holy Spirit like? What are His personality, attributes and traits? How does He flow through the life of the believer and how do we access His energies?

To know Christ is to know His Spirit.

Our misunderstanding of the Spirit's functions and interaction is usually because we try to separate Him from the person of Christ. It is important to have good theology on this, and so we should turn for a moment to the topic of Spirit baptism. Pneumatology – the theology of Holy Spirit – is one of the most mysterious areas of religious studies. It is also the most varied, controversial and incomplete.

Baptism is a Greek word that simply means immersed, inundated, dunked or overwhelmed. It is not an English word in origin. In fact, the only reason we have *baptism* in our vocabulary is because of church politics. The translators of the King James Version of the Bible were faced with potential controversy if they used the word "immersion" in their Bible. Most believers were still being sprinkled with water at baptism at the time of writing their translation. Mostly the wild Anabaptist sects practiced baptism by immersion. And loads of Anabaptists were sketchy characters in the early days – burning monasteries and libraries, raping nuns, starting revolts and plundering the upper classes. Even Martin Luther despised them. With all that going on, you can see why this was a touchy subject. There were deep divisions over the issue of sprinkling versus immersion baptism at the time. Most mature believers today realize that this is a very petty issue to merit such great debate. But we don't always understand the bigger picture of what was going on at the time. At the end of the day, the King James translators decided *not* to translate *baptismo.* Hence, a Greek word was officially left in the text and therefore injected into the English language.

Now, getting to the heart of scripture, with Spirit baptism – we are simply referring to being *immersed* in Holy Spirit.

There is tremendous disagreement in the church regarding the work of Holy Spirit in the life of the believer. There is also some incredibly poor theology surrounding the baptism or *infilling* of the Spirit. On one end of the spectrum, there are *cessationists* who essentially do not believe in the continued, experiential operation of the Spirit in the life of the church. This is by far among the most foolish of notions, for how can one ignore the thousands upon thousands of healings, deliverances, prophecies, miracles, signs and wonders that are worked in the name of Jesus today? Jesus often pointed to signs as proof of God's work, although granted, the enemy can also counterfeit signs. Even if ninety-nine percent of the untold number of healings and miracles being worked today by charismatic believers are false, hyped-up or demonic – there are still untold reams of evidence to show Holy Spirit is still playing ball.

Cessationist arguments are the most easily disproved – heal one headache and their theology falls apart. But equally troublesome, on the opposite end of the spectrum, are *religious charismatics*. They assume to command such a breadth of knowledge and experience about a Spirit they barely know. Many people think they are free from religion, simply because they are "charismatic" or so-called "Spirit-filled" believers. Yet many of these are dangerously entrenched in the yeast of the Pharisees. In my own ministry, I catch more persecution and cause more controversy amongst Pentecostals and prophets than I do anyone else!

In the days of Jesus, there were primarily two religious sects: the Pharisees and the Saducees. Saducees could essentially be compared to the cessationists of today. They did not believe in many "spiritual" things, such as angels, the resurrection, etc. However, the Pharisees were quite charismatic. They believed in angels, prophecy and the supernatural. There were even Pharisee exorcists. It was these same "charismatic" Pharisees who crucified our Lord. The scriptures are likewise full of prophets who had character flaws. I am no longer impressed if someone claims to be "Spirit-filled" or "prophetic." God is not impressed with our giftings. He's impressed with the work of His Son. The cross is a major stumbling block for charismatics and non-charismatics alike.

There is such a do-it-yourself bent in many charismatic streams; they believe that holiness, miracles, healings, prophecy and so many of the Spirit's other operations are somehow dependent on our own efforts, labors, prayers and petitions. There is often a subtle de-emphasis on the work of the cross, as Calvary becomes just one stepping stone to the Spirit-filled life. But in fact, Calvary is both the foundation and the capstone to the Spirit-filled life. It is the open door by which we access the heavens. And yet all the heavens are culminated and sourced for us there. The cross is the fountainhead of our utmost pleasure, fulfillment and abundance. It was not simply an entry rite into some greater goal. Jesus hanging on the tree is forever the Dayspring from which we drink the Spirit's deep draught.

Paul never bored with preaching the glorious simplicity of the cross. When someone really gets the revelation of the bliss of the cross, they should not become a religious fundie spouting the same four-point salvation message every Sunday. No … a true revelation of the cross fills you with joy unspeakable, and the creative energies of Holy Spirit flow through you to break paradigms, exude the phenomenal and continually reveal the Son as the champion heart of the Father.

+ Foundation of the Cross

Most Christians still view the cross as a place of personal suffering and self-denial. While acknowledging the necessity of the cross, they are wont to spend little time there. The church has for centuries taught a heretical notion that Christians still have a *sin nature*. Furthermore, it is somehow our responsibility to *die daily* and somehow put this sin nature to death on the cross. This is perhaps the greatest theological error in Christendom.

According to scripture, you no longer have a sinful nature. According to the scriptures, death to self is not a lifelong process, but was a singular, mystical transaction that already took place on the cross two thousand years ago.

> *Or don't you know that all of us who were baptized into Christ Jesus were* ***baptized into His death? We were therefore buried with Him*** *through baptism into death in order that, just as Christ was raised from the dead through the Glory of the Father, we too may live a new life.*
>
> *If we have been* ***united with Him like this in His death****, we will certainly also be united with Him in His resurrection. For we know that* ***our old self was crucified with Him so that the body of sin might be done away with****, that we should no longer be slaves to sin— because anyone who has died has been freed from sin.*[84]

You were unable to kill yourself. He did it for you. You were mystically *in Christ* when He died on the cross. On the cross, the old sinful you was eradicated. The old depressed you – the old fearful, anxious self *died*. Your

---

[84] Rom. 6:3-7, NIV

critical, religious, hateful nature was put to death. Every lustful, addictive and impoverished aspect of your *old man* was killed with Christ. You don't need a million years of inner healing and deliverance sessions. All of your generational curses of the Adamic nature were put to death with the Last Adam. Everything about the old nature was put to death. Again, we read that the sinful nature (the carnal appetite with its passions and its lusts) has been cut away once and for all in the following verse:

> *In Him you were also circumcised, in the* ***putting off of the sinful nature****, not with a circumcision done by the hands of men but with the circumcision done by Christ, having been buried with Him in baptism and raised with Him through your faith in the power of God, who raised Him from the dead.*[85]

Your old nature simply does not exist anymore. A dead man does not continue to operate in sin. Why try to continually kill something that is already dead? Many people still view the cross as a place where they need to suffer – and so the cross seems depressing to them. We've been hoodwinked! Sanctification is not a lifelong process. It's a *Person*. The cross is the most *blissful* place in the universe! It was there that you were actually *set free* from suffering, because Christ did it for you. It was there that He took the bullet for you, in order to give you delight. It was there that Heaven's riches were spilled out for you. It was there that you were delivered from sin, delivered from depression and delivered from boring religion! The cross is the founda-

---

[85] Col. 2:11-12, NIV

tion for a joy-filled life! It is the source of the intoxicating wine of the New Covenant.

You will never hear us saying things like "we need to kill the flesh" or "overcome the flesh." That is utter unbelief in what Christ has already done. He has overcome the flesh. By the way, the flesh refers to two things in scripture: in a bad sense, it is the sinful nature with its appetites and lusts. The other "flesh" is just your physical body. Your physical body is not evil. Jesus had a physical body. It is the *evil desires* of humanity that Paul is talking about when he refers to flesh in a negative way. It is imperative to understand that this has been removed from you. Otherwise, you will continually be plagued by guilt and unworthiness, never able to boldly approach the throne of Grace. You will continually feel a responsibility to somehow earn Holy Spirit (an impossibility), and subconsciously, you will always feel a need to do some sort of penance.

When Paul spoke of dying daily, it was in context of the continual persecutions he faced. He literally faced death every day! It had nothing to do with a morbid act of internally killing his old man. But religion has misapplied this verse. Many scriptures have been twisted to conform to this concept of a lifelong process of killing oneself. Why would Paul try to kill something that's already dead? Once and for all, your heart has been circumcised – the old you was cut away. Aren't you glad that circumcision is not a daily process? Ouch!

Other people would point to Jesus' statement about carrying your cross everyday as justification for killing yourself. Again, we must put this into context with the rest of scripture. Your cross speaks of a willingness to follow Him and even face persecution for Him. He guarantees that anyone who follows Him will be persecuted! This does not negate the fact that *He died for you*, and by His grace, you are a new creation. You do not need to suffer under the curse of fallen humanity. He took that for you.

The problem is not that you have a sinful nature. The problem is that you don't realize you are new. This is why it imperative to *renew the mind* with the truth of the gospel. The good news is that you died, and now you are one hundred percent new. Not just a new version of the old you. You are completely new in kind  and quality. A supernatural child of God fused into a whole new world – a whole new paradigm. In fact, *you* don't even exist anymore as an independent self. You have died, and now Christ lives in you.[86] You are actually in a whole different parallel dimension of *Heaven on Earth.* You are now seated in heavenly places. You are the righteousness of God. You are a citizen of Heaven. In Song of Solomon 4:7 He says of you, *"All beautiful you are, my darling; there is **no flaw** in you."*

Believe that you are sinless and you will manifest no sin. Believe that you have been made righteous, and you will live a righteous life. Believe it first, and you will manifest it. Stop thinking that holiness is a process of self-ascent. It was given to you once and for all as a gift.

[86] See Gal. 2:20

+ SECOND WORK VS. THE FINISHED WORK

What I am saying is that Holy Spirit is fully there in you, thanks to your union with Christ. And that union was accomplished fully on the cross.

Holy Spirit does not come to live in you, thanks to a "second work." There is one work, and it is the *finished work* of Jesus Christ on the cross. The Bible does not support a two-stage conversion process, by which something must be added to the cross. The baptism of Holy Spirit comes as a result of the cross, where the Spirit was, is and forever will be poured out.

The Spirit dwells in us permanently because of faith in the Son of God. There are also dynamic "fillings" or "baptisms" that are ancillary to this continuous, internal relationship with the Spirit of Jesus that we already have. Again, baptism literally means "immersion." In baptism, the Spirit can overwhelm, submerge you and overtake you. But He's with you all along as a believer. The more we believe, the more we *experience* our existing infilling.

Spirit *baptism* is an experiential manifestation of something we already have in Christ.

There are a number of theological viewpoints surrounding the reception, purpose and proof of Holy Spirit in the life of the believer. People have long wondered – is the Spirit given at the point of repentance and faith? That is to say, does He come at the point of conversion? John Wesley and others pointed to a "second blessing" after salvation in which the Spirit or His gifts were conferred. For Wesley, the purpose of the Spirit was to somehow "sanctify" the soul. In the early church, fathers such as Origen and Tertullian made room for post-conversion laying on of hands for imparting the Spirit – another "second blessing" type of experience.

Catholic and Orthodox believers, along with many liturgical Protestants, lean more toward a *sacramental view*, that Holy Spirit is first imparted at the ritual of water baptism. Of course, scriptures do paint a clear difference between baptism by Spirit and water. John the Baptist struck a clear difference between the two. And most will agree that outward signs of piety can have little to do with a true interior work of grace. Baptism with water does not indicate a true regeneration of heart.

The church father Augustine endorsed spiritual regeneration at conversion, but also made room for anointing after baptism. Cyril believed in a "mystical chrism" that followed and somehow *completed* baptism.[87]

When we look at the case of the disciples in the first two chapters of Acts, they were filled with Holy Spirit after being instructed by Jesus to wait for several days in Jerusalem. It would appear, therefore, that this infilling was not immediate, but subsequent to their belief in Him.

> *And being assembled together with them, He commanded them not to depart from Jerusalem, but to wait for the Promise of the Father, "which," He said, "you have heard from Me; for John truly bap-*

[87] Donald Bloesch, *The Holy Spirit: Works & Gifts* (Downers Grove, IL: InterVarsity Press, 2000).

tized with water, but you shall be baptized with the Holy Spirit not many days from now." Therefore, when they had come together, they asked Him, saying, "Lord, will You at this time restore the Kingdom to Israel?" And He said to them, "It is not for you to know times or seasons which the Father has put in His own authority.[88]

The problem in every belief system seems to be this one: we are focusing on the *time element*, rather than the person of Christ. Instead of asking "when?" we should be asking "who?" Every Holy Spirit baptism is *future tense* from the vantage point of the cross. In the same way, every salvation is future tense. We are all looking backward in time with the eyes of faith. Like the disciples of old, our questions about times and seasons are often misplaced. The key is not *when* the Lord is going to do a thing – whether at conversion, or at a later date. The question should be about *where* does it come from and *who* does it come from. He was the lamb who was slain from the foundation of the world. You have to know that Holy Spirit pours out of Christ on the cross – for He is the Spirit of Christ. As for the logistics of when we get inundated, that is not for us to worry about, as *it is not for you to know times or seasons which the Father has put in His own authority.*

The issue is to believe the cross has secured the Ghost.

+ A Living Pneumatology

Spirit baptism is not an issue of timing or formulas, nor is the laying on of hands the issue that really counts. It

[88] Acts 1:4-7, NKJV

is *faith* that causes us to access the things of the Spirit.

Holy Spirit can come upon people in various ways, in any manner of time He chooses. In Acts 8, the people of Samaria were water baptized and believed in the *name of Jesus*, but the Spirit had not yet *come upon them* until Peter and John laid hands on them. It is quite likely that they were "professing" belief, yet they had not fully received Christ. Just before Phillip arrived, these same people were following Simon the sorcerer, calling him "The Great Power." So they were likely a crowd who were impressed by Phillip's greater miracles. If they had wholeheartedly received Christ, then they would have received the Spirit already, because "if any man have not the Spirit of Christ, he is none of His."[89]

I was personally baptized in the Spirit as a backslidden, professing Christian while on an acid trip! I immediately began preaching to my drug buddies. There was no one around laying hands on me. Some time after that, I went into a charismatic church and came forward for prayer. The evangelist asked me, "Have you ever been baptized in the Spirit?" Of course, I had been radically filled – and by this point had already been literally arrested and locked up for my faith! But there was never a laying on of hands, nor had I received a formal prayer from anyone. And so, I answered him, "Not'officially." The answer seemed so funny that everyone laughed at me! The evangelist laid his hand on me and I was radically filled again!

---

[89] See Rom. 8:9

Holy Spirit can do it however He would like. He is not a little dove that is locked in a cage of theological rules. He is spontaneous and free. His dancing hand moves upon whomever He will, whenever He will. For those who wish to understand the Spirit's ways, this single verse contains perhaps the most concise pneumatological explanation as any other in the Bible:

> *The wind blows where it chooses, and you hear its sound, but you do not know where it comes from or where it is going. So is it with every one who has been born of the Spirit.*[90]

Do we receive the Spirit at salvation, or as a second work? The answer is *yes!* All of these understandings are right. We should be receiving the Spirit fresh every day! I believe the Lord is most grieved when we limit Him to a "one-time" encounter scenario – whether a one- or two-step program of Spirit baptism – that's missing the point. It's like the Samaritan woman at the well asking *where* to worship, and she doesn't even know *whom* to worship. The real issue is about intimacy with Him. We are instructed by the apostle Paul not to desire a single immersion experience, but to be continually inundated – *keep on being filled with the Spirit.*[91]

Abiding is about continually drinking from our life source. How do we continually drink of the Spirit? Because the cross forever put us into union with Him.

---

90 John 3:8, WEY
91 Eph. 5:18, ISV

We should remember that the cross is a continual, supernatural place that stands outside of time and space. It was on the cross that Jesus broke the bondage on the seasons and released a door of eternity, which we call *everlasting life*. The cross is a real and present place for us every day – not a one-time conversion rite. We are continually filled as we continually drink from Immanuel's veins. This is why we keep the feast.

+ ACCESSING THE SPIRIT

Ultimately, if we do not recognize Christ's broken body as our access point for drinking in this new wine of the New Covenant, then our foundation will be weak and shallow. I believe that Christ is the golden bowl that Zechariah saw in His vision, pouring the oil of bliss into the lampstand. Without a grace revelation of the completed work of the cross, we will attempt all sorts of strange *charismatic voodoo* in order to somehow be filled. Many people attempt many things in an effort to "spiritually advance" or deepen their walk with the Lord – instead of simply believing Jesus has already advanced us right up to Daddy's lap!

Beware of strange and unusual rites, formulas and programs that attempt to bring you closer to God or somehow get you *more filled* with the Spirit than you already are. This is not to say Holy Spirit doesn't provoke you to do strange and unusual things at times. The Spirit-filled life is extremely enigmatic and otherworldly. Strange behavior is the heavenly norm.

Here is the point: We do not do strange things *in order to access* the Spirit. Jesus is our access. However, unusual behavior can be a legitimate *byproduct* of the complete union we have with Him. Out of that realm flow many holy oddities! This is a subtle but very important distinction to make. There is a reason that these byproducts are called *manifestations*. They are simply outward derivatives of a free, inward experience of grace.

For example, I may be inundated by the Spirit and begin shaking on the floor. This is valid. But I do not shake on the floor in order to get inundated by the Spirit. This can be voodoo. Shaking does not open the heavens, Christ did. The good thing about this, is that I know Heaven is open all the time, whether I feel like it is or not. Christ once and for all tore the veil. So all I need to do is believe that I am already in – which I am – and guess what? I begin to experience it! Faith is my connector for experiencing the open Heaven I already have.

Let's make this even more practical. … However, you should be warned … the following examples are likely to offend the reader, because all of us have probably done one or more of the following things (and perhaps you are doing them right now)! As some have dubbed me a "hyper-charismatic," I believe I have some freedom to address a few common problems in our stream:

1) Some people think that by fasting, they will be filled with the Spirit. Wrong! Because of the cross you have union with the Spirit. Old Testament folks fasted a lot more than you, but they didn't get the promise. There is a popular fasting movement happening these days, and while we appreciate the passion and hunger in the hearts of these guys, a lot of it is just a trendy

new package for charismatic religion. If you enjoy fasting, please continue to do it as much as you want! We don't oppose fasting. But *true* fasting needs to be defined. Even in the Old Testament, Jesus spoke about a *better fast*, that had to do with issues of the heart, not food. I fast lots of things: *depression, religion, poverty, devils, sickness* and *boring meetings!* When questioned why His disciples did not fast, Jesus said, "How can the guests of the bridegroom fast while He is with them?"[92] Jesus also said that His disciples *would* fast, when He was taken away from them. Well … according to the scriptures, that lasted about three days! Now the Bridegroom is continually with us, dwelling inside us. Christianity is a feast, not a fast! We are feasting on the Lamb who was slain. Do not fast food unless you are feasting on Heaven. Paul warns the Colossians against those who appeal to asceticism for their spirituality.

2) Many people feel that a large amount of prayer will get them filled with the Spirit. Wrong! Jesus fills you with the Spirit. Of course, some would say, "Yes, of course it all comes from Jesus. But aren't things like prayer and fasting channels through with Jesus can work?" Sure He can. But the point is that there is freedom, and that these practices are not requirements, performance-based, nor are you going to somehow earn something from God that you don't already have. Prayer should not be some kind of faithless, repetitive banging of your head against

[92] Mark 2:19, NIV

a wall twenty-four hours a day, asking God to do a job He has already finished. Jesus warned us about praying like the pagans do. Faith prayer is a *believing* prayer. The highest prayer is worship, which is *love prayer*. Prayer is not limited simply to petitions. Paul tells us to pray continually. He did not mean you have to speak in tongues or pray for the president twenty-four hours a day. The only way you can pray continually is to effortlessly practice the Presence of God. If you are walking in an awareness of His tangible Glory all day long, then you are praying all day long. Verbal prayer is just one small part. Do not make a work out of prayer. And don't take your role as an intercessor too seriously. Like the Sabbath, prayer was given *for you to enjoy*. He doesn't need it. It helps you get things off your chest and begin to trust Him to deal with them. Believe it or not, He knows what's going on and He's got the whole world in His hands. God is on the throne.

3) Many people think that the laying on of hands will get them filled with the Spirit. Wrong! Jesus fills you with the Spirit. Does Jesus use the laying on of hands? Of course He does! But it is not the minister's hand that is doing the job. It is the resident anointing there that is activated *by faith*. If you have faith that Christ has already poured Himself out, then you do not need a man to lay hands on you. You can begin to drink from the open Heaven of the cross all day long, right where you are at. Sometimes the faith of the minister activates the anointing, and sometimes the faith of the recipient activates it. But

> nevertheless, someone is *believing*. Faith can be given away as a gift, and you can join together and partake in someone else's faith. Likewise, you can give your faith away. It is transferrable. While we should recognize the principle of the laying on of hands, and never neglect it – it is important to remember the overarching principle that it is someone's faith in Christ that is actually releasing the blessing. It is not that I am trying to sound like a stickler on this point, but people really do get dependent on ministers for their drinks. I minister in many places where the drunken Glory fills the service powerfully, but after I leave, people dry up and go back to business as usual. During the meeting they were pulling on my anointing. But if they do not understand *where I pull my anointing from*, then they will always be dependent on me. I have never lifted one finger of work for my anointing. I drink it all effortlessly from the finished work of the cross. I believe that the cross was enough to effortlessly transform me, completely fill me and absolutely perfect me. I am not a sinner anymore, but instead, I am right here, right now submerged in the creamy butterfat of Heaven's bliss!

This list could go on. Some people think they are going to reach *a new level* by introducing all new manner of good practices and disciplines into their life. Charismatics are great at coming up with new trends to improve spiritual growth. Some think that by blowing a shofar on seven mountaintops they are somehow going to take their city for Jesus. They come up with new anointing oil ingredients that will bring a better breakthrough. Or by waving their worship banners in a new way, somehow they can open the heavens in a church service. Some feel that unless they receive an impartation from the trendiest new mesmerizing speaker on the conference circuit, they will miss God. I even know a prominent charismatic minister today who goes so far as to say that *sonship* is some type of special anointing that you must attain through a unique impartation. Of course, if *this speaker* mentors or lays hands on you, perhaps you can get it and become a son of God. Where does the madness end?

Let me say that you are already in the creamy center of Heaven right now. Ephesians 2:6 tells us that we are already seated in heavenly places. This is not "positional" make-believe. It is reality. You do not open the heavens through any efforts of your own. The heavens are not opened because the worship leader hit a great riff during last Sunday's music set. Heaven is opened because the veil of Christ's flesh was torn. He is the one who made us to be the spiritual seed of Abraham, and therefore, the seed of God. Many ministers will give you steps as to how they received their anointing, so that you can try to do the same thing and get the same results like an algebra formula: *I prayed twelve hours a day! I did seven forty-day fasts! I chose not to marry! I refrain from eating pork!*

At the end of the day, you will rarely hear the truth … that everything these ministers received came as a *gift*. It was no effort of their own that secured the anointing for them. It was grace. Never feel a pressure to fit someone else's mold, in order to copy their results. No strife or effort of their own achieved them their anointing.

CHAPTER TWO

But one and the same Spirit works all these things, distributing to each one individually as ***He wills***.[93]

In terms of strange practices, some would ask, "Isn't Crowder calling the kettle black?" After all, it does not take much research on YouTube before one sees me doing all sorts of seemingly obnoxious antics from pretend smoking baby Jesus dolls to wearing Mexican luchador outfits in church. Some who have only read my books, but never been to one of our meetings, may be expecting *only* logical teachings when I take to the pulpit. But in person, my demeanor and orthopraxy is a bit … well … unusual.

First of all, much of this is just "inspired" joking. But as I said earlier, manifestations can be *extremely* unusual – as can prophetic acts. Isaiah walked naked for years. Ezekiel cooked with dung cakes. Jesus spat on people. In a similar way, God has put a *signs prophet* mantle on us, in which we – in the midst of having fun in the Glory – inadvertently *act out* many of our messages. I am fully aware that the things I do are construed as absolute craziness. But in actuality, we are just having fun in God's presence. We enjoy the happy presence of God and people get free from religion, so they stop taking themselves so seriously. Freedom from pride is liberating and empowering. The Lord loves to mock religion through us, because religion grieves Him tremendously.

What we are *never* doing is trying to make a formula out of these crazy antics. In fact, most of these antics are gloriously deriding religious formula!

---

93 1 Cor. 12:11, NKJV

Our antics are so crazy in fact that you would have to be a complete nutjob to think smoking a baby Jesus doll is the latest tool to get you to a *new level* with God. These silly acts don't get us filled with the Spirit, nor are we trying to start a new denomination with this stuff. We do lots of fun, goofy things because we *are already in the Spirit* by His grace, and we've been set free from the performance-oriented version of Christianity. Enigmatic behavior is normative for believers, but let it all be a responsive act of joy for what Christ has done – never an effort to appear spiritual, get His approval or gain entrance to His courts. Likewise, it's never just to cause trouble or be intentionally divisive. It's just that fun needs to be recovered to Christendom.

+ THE QUEST FOR ASSURANCE

As we are now talking about manifestations of the Spirit, we should briefly address the topic of *evidence* or signs that accompany the Spirit-filled life. This seems necessary for a well-rounded discussion about Holy Spirit, before we return to the specific "sevenfold" aspect of His operations.

In the latter half of the nineteenth century many reformed Protestants, primarily Holiness Movement advocates, began looking for some certainty of their reception of Holy Spirit. They wanted proof – external evidence that the Spirit had been imparted to them. Due to the invisible, often intangible nature of the Spirit, this quest seemed rather elusive.
The Wesleyan Holiness stream had a long history of wild, ecstatic experience from its roots in Methodism. Early Methodist meetings were quite "fanatical" in that

regard. But as the baptism of the Spirit grew to a national topic of discussion in the late 1800s, holiness groups sought a specific sign or manifestation of the Spirit that would confirm the fact that they had indeed received it. This came to a frenzied peak by the turn of the century. There were no standards everyone agreed upon as to what the actual evidence of Holy Spirit was supposed to look like. Despite the modern fallacy that gifts and manifestations *disappeared* after the Book of Acts, the truth is that there has *never* been a period in the history of the church where the gifts were *not* present. Holiness people were quite familiar with trances, healings, shouting, dancing, tongues, visions and prophecy. All of these same manifestations happened in their churches, if not regularly, then sporadically. But no one could decide which of these manifestations was the foolproof evidence of Spirit baptism.

We should remember that society was in an age where scientific, empirical evidence was more in vogue than ever before. People wanted proof. Because of this, the holiness church was more ready than ever to embrace the Azusa Street revival with its hallmark doctrine of speaking in tongues as the gold standard "initial evidence" of Holy Spirit baptism. It is clear that the Lord used the subsequent Pentecostal movement to restore and highlight the gift of tongues to the church as a whole. But any serious scholar would be hard pressed to embrace such a quirky doctrine that tongues is the "one and only" sure fire sign of the infilling.

There is no verse that directly states that tongues is the sign of the infilling. In fact, the scriptures tell us that *not everyone* gets tongues in the church. But the Lord does come to live in all who believe, and we are all free to receive the gift of tongues if we desire it.

Lonnie Frisbee, the controversial revivalist of the Jesus People Movement in the 1970s, often quoted Bob Mumford in saying, "The real evidence of the Holy Spirit is not tongues … it's *trouble*!"[94]

For the Wesleyans, the Spirit brought a "second work" of sanctification (Wesleyans thought Holy Spirit came to give you a holy life in a separate event subsequent to salvation). There was not a proper understanding that our old nature was replaced on Christ's cross at conversion, rather than an elusive "second event." It is true that the Spirit enables us to walk in holiness, because His nature becomes our nature, but the exchange happens at salvation. Nevertheless, because people put their *faith* toward God for holiness, He did give them the manifest experience of it.

But now, with the advent of Azusa Street, Pentecostals made a systematic separation from the Wesleyans before them. The Pentecostals now spoke of a "third blessing" of sorts – officially calling it the *baptism of the Holy Spirit* which had the purpose of empowering the believer for the winning of souls and the work of ministry. This *third blessing* was not about holiness, but about power.

In the early days of the Pentecostal Holiness movement, there was a popular three-step approach for believers: salvation, sanctification and Spirit baptism. Eventually,

---

[94] Quote comes from former Frisbee friend and associate Peter Crawford.

this mushroomed into all sorts of strange sequenced events, because the "third blessing" just wasn't enough. One of the early holiness preachers, Benjamin Irwin, founder of the Fire-Baptized Holiness Association, advocated up to six or seven different baptisms. There was, of course, the *baptism of fire*, hence the namesake. But the constant need for something more phenomenal led to the baptism of dynamite, lyddite and oxidite, just to name a few. There were actually loads of people who got into this stuff!

"Those receiving 'the fire' would often shout, scream, speak in other tongues, fall into trances, and even get the 'jerks,'" writes holiness movement historian Vinson Synan.[95] We can't fault Irwin for his hunger, and truly it appears that the Lord moved mightily among them – not because of their theology, but in spite of it.

Protestants were not the only ones who moved toward a "second experience." Catholics and Eastern Orthodox began implementing the sacrament of "confirmation" as far back as the fourth century, in which they believe that the Spirit is poured out on them either as a seal or *confirmation* of their salvation, or as a point of moving into the gifts of the Spirit. Granted, in most Catholic circles it is a mere formalism followed by an after party. But the principle is still adhered to that Holy Spirit has to come at a point *after* salvation.

At the moment of faith, Holy Spirit seals us. Some are "inundated" or "immersed" in a tangible way, immediately at the moment of conversion. For others, the feel-

---

95 Vinson Synan, *The Holiness-Pentecostal Movement in the United States* (Grand Rapids: William B. Eerdmans Publishing Co., 1971), 62.

ing of His Presence, the experience of a manifestation or some other phenomena of His presence overwhelm them at some point afterward. For some, it comes with the laying on of hands. For some, God has invaded their lives spontaneously, taking them by surprise. Still others live their whole lives, wanting an experience and never receiving one. There are no formulas to the baptism or filling of the Spirit. Holy Spirit is not turned on or off like a sacramental switch. In every one of these cases, the issue hinges on *faith.* And you can't work faith up. Even that comes as a gift of grace.

A lot of people in a lot of movements have diligently searched for "signs" to prove the indwelling presence of Holy Spirit. But I might put forward the recommendation that this has been altogether backward. Holy Spirit *is* the sign – He is the seal of conversion. Signs don't point to Holy Spirit; rather, Holy Spirit points us to Jesus. He is the *Spirit of Jesus*.

> *And you also were included in Christ when you heard the word of truth, the gospel of your salvation. Having believed, you were marked in Him with a seal, the promised Holy Spirit.*[96]

Most liturgical streams had always considered acts of service to be proof of the infilling. A lifestyle of good character was the sign. This is true, good and vital. But it is also too easily mimicked by natural human morality. Good ole boys in the south all claim to be Christians. Buddhists are more moral than many American Christians. They detest pornography, thievery, gluttony, etc. If there is to be an evidential sign of the Spirit, it

---

[96] Eph. 1:13, NIV

must necessarily be beyond human ability to accomplish. It must be supernatural. The East Syrian Christian mystic Abdisho Hazzaya, in the seventh century, said the first sign of Holy Spirit's presence in the life of a believer is the love of God that "burns in the heart of a person like fire."[97] This is perhaps closest to the truth.

Nevertheless, the search for evidence is really putting the cart before the horse. As reformed believers, we do not need to pursue evidence of our right standing in the sight of God. *Faith itself* (which means trust or dependence) is the assurance that we are accepted and loved by God through the sacrifice of His Son. That faith will manifest in a variety of ways. But the faith comes first.

The pursuit of manifestations and signs can be admittedly wrong if it stems from a desire for personal proof of acceptance. Look at Jesus hanging on the tree and that should be proof positive of His love for you. However, the eager desire for the Spirit's gifts and miraculous phenomena is perfectly legitimate for the pure enjoyment of the saints and as a necessary power for witness. *Signs and wonders must accompany the gospel.* Signs will follow a life of intimacy. But the reverse is not necessarily true. Signs themselves are not necessarily an indicator of intimacy.

It is difficult to theologically justify a two-step or three-step program. The Spirit is given at true salvation. One all-sufficient step. But are there many baptisms? If baptism is merely to be *inundated*, then inundate me every day! Be filled continually. Holy Spirit is a person, and we are to have a continual relationship with Him. He

---

97 Bloesch, *The Holy Spirit: Works & Gifts*, 55.

came fully as a gift at salvation, and every day is a fresh influx as we hang on the wine vine. Experiential activation into this Gift of God is a lifelong process of discovering our bliss.

And what is the salvific role of Holy Spirit? He is not making us more and more holy than we already are, but He is truly renewing us inwardly in the sense that He is always reminding us of Jesus. The Blood of Jesus has transformed us, and Holy Spirit is continually unwrapping this reality before our eyes. Experientially, *in practice*, the Spirit is enabling us to operate in the reality of this gift of holiness in our daily lives. Even better than that – He is doing it through us! God doesn't *help* you. He does it for you. Unlike the striving, straining sector of our charismatic movement, you will never hear me praying things like "Make us holy!" He wants us to believe the gospel – that He has already done that. I do not beg Him for the fullness of His Spirit. He says I already have it. This is faith-based, not evidentiary.

In all our desire for evidence, it must be remembered, "*blessed are those who have not seen and yet have believed.*"[98]

Like an almond tree, you are growing and waking up to who you are and what is inside of you. When your buds open and your blossoms are fully flowering with the revelation of His Word, then the Spirit will manifest brighter and brighter in your life.

---

[98] See John 20:29

CHAPTER TWO

+ The Revelation of Fullness

If you want to manifest the fullness of Holy Spirit, it is vital that you believe He is fully inside of you. Manifestation is effortless. A revelation of the truth is what is needed.

Revelation brings faith – you can't believe something unless you hear it. Faith comes by hearing.

Never think you lack fullness simply because you are not manifesting it a certain way. Instead, be saturated by the Word of truth regarding the matter. Colossians 2:10 says, "You have been given fullness in Christ, who is the head over every power and authority."[99]

Rest in the truth of the Word, and be daily drenched with a fresh anointing like the dew on Mt. Hermon. Like the pipes of Zechariah, you have been given an unlimited flow of the river of His Spirit. Like the widow of Zarephath who believed Elijah, we are called first to believe the Lord – then comes the manifestation of a jar of oil that never runs dry.[100]

The presence of problems or difficult life circumstances do not indicate the existence of lack.

Base your life on the Word, rather than your problems. Be established in the revelation of the cross, knowing that the Father has already "blessed us in the heavenly realms with every spiritual blessing in Christ."[101] This

---

[99] Col. 2:10, NIV
[100] See 1 Kings 17
[101] See Eph. 1:3

revelation of the word is necessary to shine forth all the fullness we've been given.

Revelation is not a mental understanding of the word, but a heart-level belief. A lot of people claim to believe the Bible cover to cover. They even have it memorized. But theirs is simply a cognitive, intellectual agreement with the word. It is not a deep-seated belief of the heart.

The apostle Paul wanted us to "know this love that surpasses knowledge—that you may be filled to the measure of all the fullness of God."[102] The knowledge of His love causes the fullness of God to shine forth in us. Although Paul says we have already been given God's fullness, he also says we are given ministers so that we might be "attaining to the whole measure of the fullness of Christ."[103] This attaining is not a work, nor an admission that you lack fullness already. It is simply an activation of faith that comes when His servants "present to you the word of God in its fullness."[104] A full revelation of the Word brings a full manifestation of the Spirit.

What does this mean? Believe you are full, thanks to Christ, and you will be what you really are ... full!

As we mature in our spirituality, that fullness which we *already possess* begins to break forth from our lives in its *whole measure.* Maturity is loving God and believing the Word. In this place, we truly begin to demonstrate those realms of *all things are possible.*

---

[102] See Eph. 3:19
[103] See Eph. 4:13
[104] See Col. 1:25

+ CHAPTER THREE
THE SEVEN EYES OF GOD

Now that we have laid some foundational pneumatology, we are free to explore deeper the sevenfold river of Holy Spirit flowing through the life of the church. This abundance of oil runs through us and burns in the church as lamps of fire – the seven eyes of the Lord. But we have yet to discover exactly what are these seven Spirit's of God? Our answer is found in the Book of Isaiah:

A shoot will come up from the stump of Jesse;
From His roots a Branch will bear fruit.

And the ***Spirit of the Lord*** *shall rest upon Him,*
The Spirit of ***Wisdom*** *and* ***Understanding****,*
The Spirit of ***Counsel*** *and* ***Might,***
The Spirit of ***Knowledge*** *and of the* ***Fear of the Lord****.*[105]

The seven Spirits of God are listed here. The first is the *Spirit of the Lord.* This is literally the Spirit of *Jehovah.* Remembering back to our lampstand picture, this would be the center pipe, out of which all the other six branches flow. The center pipe is not about what He does – it is about *who He is*! It is the *Spirit of Adonai.* Following this first and center pipe are the other six flows of the Spirit: Wisdom, Understanding, Counsel, Might (or *Power*), Knowledge and the Fear of the Lord.

Important note! These following six Spirits come listed in *pairs*:

The Spirit of Wisdom ***and*** Understanding

---

105 Isa. 11:1-2, KJV

The Spirit of Counsel ***and*** Might
The Spirit of Knowledge ***and*** of the Fear of the Lord

In the same way, the six mirrored branches of the menorah come out of the center shaft in *pairs of two*. The patterns of two are demonstrated in the diagram below, with the center shaft alone in the middle.

D---C---B----A----B---C---D

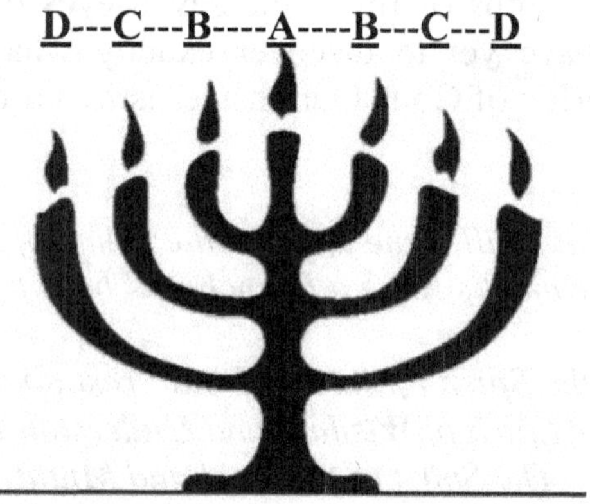

A- Spirit of the Lord
B- Wisdom and Understanding
C- Counsel and Might
D- Knowledge and the Fear of the Lord

+ Branches in Pairs

The seven branches of the lampstand are all one piece, just as His sevenfold nature is still one Spirit. The six branches flowing out from the center shaft represent God's agency through mankind. Six is the number of man. Man was created on the sixth day. Only by abiding in the vine – by staying connected to the center pipe, is man made complete. Seven is the number of perfection. We are the branches that abide in Him, because apart from Him, we can do nothing. The center lamp, the Spirit of the Lord, is about His name, while the other six branches represent His outworking through us. He is the center pipe inside of a believer supplying the oil.

The name of Jesus is an oil that anoints and ordains every believer for ministry. The Shulamite says of Him, "*Your name is oil poured out.*"[106] All the other functions of the Spirit through mankind are sourced in the name of Christ, the Anointed One.

There is a reason that the six secondary lamps are listed in pairs. This is because each of them works closely in tandem with a partner. Some overlap so closely, you can barely tell a difference between them. For instance, wisdom and understanding are so similar, you can hardly tell them apart. The counsel of God always releases the might of God. And you cannot rightly have the fear of the Lord unless it is properly paired with the intimate knowledge of God. The pairs work together.

In the next chapters, we will look at these Spirits independently. But I have paired them in each chapter to further discuss how they work both together and individually.

+ Spirit of the Lord: The Center Pipe

We see in Isaiah 11 that Jesus, the Branch of Jesse, was anointed with this sevenfold Spirit of God. This is yet another confirmation that we are not merely speaking of seven angels. This is the authority in

[106] Song of Sol. 1:3, ESV

which Christ operated in His earthly ministry. The church works with angels, but the oil of anointing flowing through the lamp of the church is God Himself, our source.

This passage in Isaiah does bear resemblance to another passage in the same book, by which Jesus first revealed His identity and authority in the synagogue of Nazareth quoting:

> *The Spirit of the Lord is on me, because He has anointed me to preach good news to the poor. He has sent me to proclaim freedom for the prisoners and recovery of sight for the blind, to release the oppressed, to proclaim the year of the Lord's favor.*[107]

This is the Spirit without measure that rested on Christ. Because the Spirit of the Lord is now within you, you share in His authority as a co-regent to preach good news to the poor, liberate captives, give sight to the blind, break oppression and proclaim an eternal year of the Lord's favor.

The Spirit of the Lord flows through us only because we are grafted into the Vine. Jesus bore no notion of false humility in acknowledging His divinity. He was of the *Spirit of the Lord.* Jesus never refused personal worship when men recognized His divinity on Earth. He once rebuked His disciples in saying, "*You do not know what manner of spirit you are of.*"[108] However, Jesus always knew the Spirit to whom He belonged.

---

107 Luke 4:18-19; Isa. 61:1, NIV

108 See Luke 9:55

Because He was firmly established in His identity as the Son of God, the tempter in the wilderness, who incessantly sought to provoke Him to doubt never toppled Him with the challenge: *If You really are the Son of God. ...*

+ THE BRANCH OF JESSE

One of the most beautiful names of Jesus is the Branch of Jesse. This is how He is described, as the One upon whom the sevenfold would rest. Most specifically, this relates to Christ's humanity, from the lineage of David, Jesse's son.

The Hebrew word for "branch" is *netser* and is not a glamorous word. It means *sucker*. It's the unwanted sprout that springs up from a chopped down tree.[109] Have you ever seen the shoots trying to grow up again from the stump of a tree? They are usually considered *weeds*.

Christ laid aside His heavenly Glory, stepped into the Earth as a lowly, despised man. In fact, He sprang up from the cut down tree of David's family. When Christ stepped into creation, He did so at one of Israel's lowest points in history under Roman occupation. The royal authority of the house of David and Solomon had been cut down from its former golden age, having lain dormant for six hundred years. Isaiah prophesied that the house of David would be cut down like a mighty tree, for its pride.

---

[109] H.D.M. Spence and Joseph Exell, ed., *The Pulpit Commentary: Isaiah*, Vol. 1 (New York: Funk & Wagnalls Co., 1950), 214.

But God chose to bring life again from this long-dead stump - a prophetic symbol of resurrection power came forth in this meager shoot. Lowly, born in manger, Christ came into the world amid humble beginnings. Is it no wonder that He asks Zerubbabel in the lampstand passage of Zechariah 4, "For who has despised the day of small things?"[110]

Christ *grew up* as the branch. He *grew in wisdom and stature, and in favor with God and men.*[111] He was always perfect. Always without sin. Yet He matured. Did you know that God loves you, even in your immaturity? Immaturity is not evil, but according to your age and ability. Babies can be perfect for their age. In the same way, you are perfect in Christ, though you are still growing in many areas. A baby shoot and a mighty oak have one thing in common: *they are both trees.* In the same way, you have the same holy God-DNA of your Father. You have not grown into your full stature yet, but you have the same seed and substance within you. The little branches grow up to reign as mighty kings.

> *"The days are coming," says Adonai, "when I will raise a righteous Branch for David. He will reign as king and succeed, He will do what is just and right in the land. In His days Y'hudah will be saved, Isra'el will live in safety, and the name given to Him will be Adonai Tzidkenu [Adonai our righteousness]."*[112]

Jesus the *sucker shoot* drank of the same nutrients as

---

110 Zech. 4:10, NKJV

111 Luke 2:52, NIV

112 Jer. 23:5-6, CJB

Jesse. As the Bride of Christ, you are the vine grafted into His side. You drink of that same substance of the Spirit of Life. Just as Eve came from Adam's side, so have you sprung forth from His opened side. Just as the blood and water poured from His body for our betrothal, likewise we now drink of His essence as we are grafted into the menorah.

Jesus, the branch, came from Judah. This was a kingly tribe. You too are a little shoot springing out from Him. This was a prophecy for Judah given in Genesis 49:

> *The sceptre shall not depart from Judah, nor a lawgiver from between his feet. ... Binding his foal unto the vine, and his ass's colt unto the choice vine; he washed his garments in wine, and his clothes in the blood of grapes: his eyes shall be red with wine (lit. bloodshot with wine), and his teeth white with milk.*[113]

Did you know that you are a little ass tied to the Vine? You are like the donkey Jesus rides into Jerusalem. Don't despise your own day of small beginnings! You may seem to be an ass, but you have Jesus riding on you! You are literally *tied to the wine vine*! Not just any vine – but the choice one that sprouts wine grapes. And Christ's own eyes are bloodshot from drinking this Holy Spirit wine of divine intimacy!

+ THE LAMPS OF THE LORD

Remember that the seven Spirits are the lamps that rest *on top* of the lampstand – not the stand itself. They pro-

[113] Gen. 49:10-12, KJV, my note

vide illumination to the word, just as they continually shone upon the table of shewbread in the temple. In the same way, Holy Spirit always points us to Jesus, and His lamps shine upon Him who is seated upon the throne.

> *And out of the throne proceeded lightnings and thunderings and voices: and there were* ***seven lamps of fire burning before the throne****, which are the* ***seven Spirits of God.***[114]

Jesus is the Light of the World, given off by the Menorah, just as we, the branches, are likewise called to be the light of the world, shining Him forth.[115] Remember that John the Revelator also says that these seven Spirits are *eyes*:

> *And I beheld, and, lo, in the midst of the throne and of the four beasts, and in the midst of the elders, stood a Lamb as it had been slain, having seven horns and* ***seven eyes, which are the seven Spirits of God sent forth into all the Earth****.*[116]

This Lamb is the same man John saw at the beginning of His book, among the lampstands, who was like a son of man, and His *eyes were like blazing fire.*[117] Daniel, centuries before John, saw this same man with *eyes as lamps of fire.*[118] Furthermore, remember the words of Jesus as He taught that the eye is the lamp of the body:

---

[114] Rev 4:5, KJV
[115] See John 8:12; Matt. 5:14
[116] Rev. 5:6, KJV
[117] See Rev. 1:13-14
[118] See Dan. 10:6

THE SEVEN EYES OF GOD

> *The eye is the lamp of the body. If your eyes are good, your whole body will be full of light.*[119]

Spiritually, eyes are considered to be fiery lamps. Furthermore, wherever your eye is turned, there your spirit is turned as well. We gaze at what we love. And what we gaze upon is the thing we become. You are what you see, and you become what you love. Gazing upon Christ makes us like Him, as John the love disciple says, "But we know that when He appears, we shall be like Him, for we shall see Him as He is."[120]

It is not with our natural eyes, but with our spirits that we truly see. The flaming, all-seeing eyes of the Lord are continually wandering through the Earth, ministering to His bride:

> *For the eyes of the Lord range throughout the Earth to strengthen those whose hearts are fully committed to Him.*[121]

Again, we see these seven Spirit eyes scouting the Earth in Zechariah's vision:

> *For these seven rejoice to see the plumb line in the hand of Zerubbabel. They are the eyes of the Lord which scan to and fro throughout the whole Earth.*[122]

Holy Spirit does a number of things by means of these

---

[119] Matt. 6:22, NIV

[120] 1 John 3:2, NIV

[121] 2 Chron. 16:9, NIV

[122] Zech. 4:10, NKJV

roving, watching lamps. For one, the Lord inspects His church. He tells the church at Thyatira that He is the one "who searches the minds and the hearts."[123] And in Proverbs we read of Him shining on individuals as "The lamp of the Lord searches the spirit of a man; it searches out his inmost being."[124]

Another job description of a lamp is to bring illumination into darkened places. He reveals all things. But this is far more than revealing sin or wickedness, for this is not the Spirit's primary intent in the life of a believer. The Spirit comes to reveal the heart of the Father:

> *The Spirit searches all things, even the deep things of God.*[125]

The lamps of the Lord shine on Jesus, not sinfulness.

+ No More Sin Focus

There are many "sin-focused" individuals in the body of Christ who feel that repentance is merely a *turning away from sin.* They feel that unless people are crying and mourning over sin, then somehow God is not at work. Many simply do not understand the basic meaning of the word "repentance," and so they assume it is merely an endless cycle of morbid introspection. When we consider the root word *pent*, it literally speaks of a *high place.* Consider our English word *penthouse.* It is the highest place in a building. Repentance is a change of mind that leads to a change of behavior. But even

---

[123] See Rev. 2:18

[124] Prov. 20:27, NIV

[125] 1 Cor. 2:10, NIV

more, it literally means to *turn back to the high place.* Turn back to Heaven. Turn back to God. Turn back to as it was in Eden! Turn back to the Glory and pleasure of God for which your life was intended.

Repentance is not and endless cycle of beating up one's self over something for which we are already forgiven. It's time we actually replace those old self-defeating, downward spirals with something glorious and worthy! Christianity has no room for a sin consciousness anymore. Only a *God consciousness.* True repentance has to do with turning back to joy, fruitfulness, kindness, gentleness and all the fruits of the Spirit! When you have a God-consciousness, you stop sinning.

This is important to discuss, because in this day and age, many Christians have been taught that Holy Spirit's only job is to *convict us of sin.* This is an unfortunate misapplication of John 16:8:

> *When He comes, He will convict the world of guilt in regard to sin. ...*[126]

My question is this: if you are a believer in Christ, are you still *of the world?* No. Holy Spirit convicts sinners of their guilt. Convict means to legally prove someone's guilt as in a court of law (i.e. convict someone of a criminal offense). You, on the other hand, as a believer, are no longer guilty. You are forgiven, and there is therefore now no condemnation for them that believe.

Of course, the light of Holy Spirit will *reveal* sin or wrong practices in the life of the believer. We should

---

[126] John 16:8, NIV

immediately feel His grief if we do something offensive to God. But Holy Spirit is so much more than a lawyer. He is the divine kiss of the Father. He is our Encourager, Comforter and Friend. Those who only know Holy Spirit as a prosecuting attorney should get saved, because there is therefore now no condemnation for those who are in Christ Jesus![127]

With this fact established, let us now understand that the lamps of the Lord are not pointing to sin, but to God. Holiness is not the absence of sin. It is the Presence of God. When God shows up, sin flees as a necessary byproduct. No sin will stand in His Presence.

In the New Jerusalem, where "the Lamb is its light," we learn that "the nations will walk by its light."[128] This New Jerusalem is us, His body – God's eternal temple where He will forever live among His people.

> *There will be no more night. They will not need the light of a lamp or the light of the sun, for the Lord God will give them light. And they will reign for ever and ever.*[129]

+ Let Your Light Shine

Christ wants the brilliancy of His Glory to radiate from an upright church, unashamedly enlightening the world with His manifold wisdom and love. When Holy Spirit infuses you with the wine of this transcendent love, a supernatural boldness enables you to boldly proclaim the Glory of God – openly and without fear. These riv-

---

[127] See Rom. 8:1

[128] See Rev. 21:23, 24

[129] Rev. 22:5, NIV

ers of oil *must* spill out of you. Your lamp – just like your Christianity – was never intended to be a *covert operation*! How many believers have been sidetracked and foiled by the notion that they somehow have been entrusted with an "undercover operation" from the Lord – a seeker sensitivity that never surfaces. They feel they must keep their faith secretive or toned down in their lives, careers and even their churches! This is rarely a true strategy from God. It is usually a sub-justification for fear.

> *No one lights a lamp and hides it in a jar or puts it under a bed. Instead, he puts it on a stand, so that those who come in can see the light.*[130]

And again we read …

> *Neither do men light a candle, and put it under a bushel, but on a candlestick; and it giveth light unto all that are in the house.* ***Let your light so shine before men****, that they may see your good works, and glorify your Father which is in Heaven.*[131]

Unfortunate as it may be, when we refuse to shine with a burning heart of passion, our lampstand can be displaced. This was the admonition given to the church of Ephesus, who had replaced their first love with works and deeds. It caused the Lord to caution them, "If you do not repent, I will come to you and remove your lampstand from its place."[132] Rather than a fearful threat, this should be a flattering gesture toward us. The

---

[130] Luke 8:16, NIV

[131] Matt. 5:15-16, KJV

[132] See Rev. 2:5

Lord is so lovingly interested in our hearts, that He would prefer us do nothing else in terms of religious duties and labors, if it distracts us from pure, intimate consideration of Him. He wants lovers.

One of the worst theological statements oft repeated by ministers is this: *One day, the honeymoon will be over!* Some make a negative prediction that after our initial betrothal at salvation, the "goose bumps" of first love will fade away. Then we will be left with a choice to dutifully follow the Lord – drumming up a sense of dull obligation void of feeling or emotion.

The scriptures say nothing about the honeymoon ending. In fact, Jesus warns here that the honeymoon *better not end!* He wants us to be continually excited and zealous for Him, as on the very first day we were ever saved. His only warning is not about a honeymoon ending – rather, He says watch out if you become lukewarm! For then He wants to spew you from His mouth.

The fire in these lamps is the fire of love. Your only purpose in this life is to have your lamp continually burning. How? By passively drinking in the oil of His presence you cannot help but burn. Fuel is added to the fire. In fact, the only way you can constantly love Him is because He constantly loves you.

> *Be dressed ready for service and keep your lamps burning, like men waiting for their master to return from a wedding banquet, so that when He comes and knocks they can immediately open the door for Him. It will be good for those servants whose master finds them watching when He comes. I tell you the truth, He will dress Himself to serve, will have*

> *them recline at the table and will come and wait on them. It will be good for those servants whose master finds them ready, even if He comes in the second or third watch of the night.*[133]

This is not the wait of boredom. Not the wait of unfulfilling servitude. This is wonderstruck wait of *expectancy* – lamp fueling trust in His good promises.

Christ is truly the only one who can keep this flame alit. He is the High Priest who tends the lampstand. You are powerless to love Him, except that He first loved you.

+ SPIRIT AND THE WORD

I believe that the two golden pipes which Zechariah saw feeding the lampstand are ultimately fulfilled as prophetic symbols of the *Spirit* and the *Word.* In these two, the church ultimately worships the Father.[134]

This dual theme of the Spirit and the Word (Truth) working together in unison is a resounding narrative in the study of the sevenfold. We will address this in more depth in the final chapter. Let us only mention here – regarding lamps – that both the Spirit and the Word of God are scripturally represented as lamps.

> *Thy word is a lamp unto my feet, and a light unto my path.*[135]

---

[133] Luke 12:35-38, NIV

[134] See John 4:23

[135] Ps. 119:105, KJV

For the commandment is a lamp and the teaching a light.[136]

The Spirit and the Word are perfectly united in the person of Christ. *The words I have spoken to you are spirit and they are life.*[137] Therefore we now partake in the full nature of Holy Spirit and the Word of God. *We are light in the Lord* and *in His light we see light.*[138]

The concept of the Lord being a *light* is perhaps one of the first revelations we ever receive as believers. John opens His gospel, calling Jesus the *light which shines in the darkness*, but the darkness has not understood it.[139] Likewise, Saul, on the Damascus road, was first converted in the blinding luminescence of Christ. But this is an ever-increasing light – a Glory that forever grows brighter. The Psalmist says, "Arise, shine, for your light has come, and the Glory of the Lord rises upon you."[140] It is the Glory of God that we radiate – and in this cloud of His presence we are consumed by divine love.

Is it no wonder that, throughout church history, believers have at times physically glowed as a light bulb? This is a miracle that has occurred numerous times in the church age, called *luminescence effluvia* by scholars. Even outward manifestations this phenomenal only mark an inward radiance of His indwelling grace. As the eyes of our spirits are overpowered with this Uncreated Light, we are blinded to all darkness. The mature Christian is no longer focused on darkness – even with

---

[136] Prov. 6:23, ESV
[137] See John 6:63
[138] See Eph. 5:8; Ps. 36:9
[139] See John 1:5
[140] See Isa. 60:1

the goal of defeating it. There was a time in our growth perhaps, when we were actively engaged in warring against the demonic. But spiritual warfare cannot properly be called such in the full revelation of His pure light. Like children we once squirted our water guns at the fires of hell with our shouts, petitions and our travailing intercession. But when faith comes, we can no longer afford to spend a spare moment, searching for devils behind every bush. Yes … the devils may exist. And yes … they may be behind every bush. But we no longer focus on them, for our eyes are full of light. And in our new world of perfect union with God, they cannot touch us. If your eye is full of light, all you see is Christ. You live in a dimension of existence where the demonic has been defeated. A place called *it is finished.* Even the bushes burn with fire.

> *Your eye is the lamp of your body. When your eyes are good, your whole body also is full of light. But when they are bad, your body also is full of darkness. See to it, then, that the light within you is not darkness. Therefore, if your whole body is full of light, and no part of it dark, it will be completely lighted, as when the light of a lamp shines on you.*[141]

Keeping our eye focused on the finished works of Christ is highly detrimental to one's paranoid, hypercharismatic "demon focus." As you walk down the street, you see nothing but Jesus. He is everywhere. You can meet the worst of sinners – prostitutes, crack addicts and thieves. But you don't see their problems. All you see is the prophetic potential of Christ being

---

[141] Luke 11:34-36, NIV

formed in their lives. In His light, we see light. Don't allow your eyes to focus on darkness, depression, demons or disease. Be raptured in a continuous gaze of love at the Bridegroom. He will expose the demonic, because in this light, *there is nothing hid, which shall not be manifested.*[142]

+ SEE THE VOICE

Spiritual sight is far deeper and *more real* than natural sight. It is based not on the physical limitations of the human eye, but on the clear understanding of God's heart of love. One of the roles of Holy Spirit is to give us practical, revelatory illumination from the scriptures. Reading your Bible is only effective when the Spirit opens it up to you. This is because Holy Spirit's eyes are always shining upon Jesus, showing Him to us on every page. The Pharisees constantly searched the scriptures, but most of them missed Christ when He came. They never saw Jesus in the scriptures, though Holy Spirit is continually directing us to Him in the Word. Consider the visual imagery in John's first encounter in the Book of Revelation. John receives a message that is not spoken, but it is *seen.* It is full of pictorial imagery. "*What you see*, write in a book and send to the seven churches. ..."[143] The next verse declares:

> *And I turned to* ***see the voice*** *that was speaking to me. ...*[144]

---

[142] See Mark 4:22

[143] Rev. 1:11, NKJV

[144] Rev. 1:12, NKJV

John saw a voice! Most people hear a voice. But there's a picture-message in the Word. What did John see? He saw the seven golden lampstands, and one "like a son of man" in their midst. The vision is a message.

This spiritual sight does not come through study, prayer or any degree of discipline. It is the gift of God. Eyes that were shrouded and blinded by sin, the law, religion – the veil is torn when we encounter Christ. This sight is Holy Spirit peering through you. He is a gift who comes freely to all who ask and believe. Christ has this pure spiritual discernment via the sevenfold Spirit that rests upon Him. The seven eyes of the Lamb enables Him to "*not judge by the sight of His (natural) eyes, nor decide by the hearing of His (natural) ears.*"[145]

How does Jesus have eyes of pure discernment? They are bathed in the Spirit. Song of Solomon says His eyes are literally "washed in milk."

> *His eyes are like doves by the water streams, washed in milk, mounted like jewels.*[146]

Holy Spirit is the dove that rested upon Christ in the river Jordan. The Spirit became His eyes. Physiologically, the dove is a bird that has no peripheral vision. Doves have tunnel vision. The bird is focused and centered on what is right before him. Focused on His Father, Christ was never distracted by fears, doubts or the intimidation of the demonic. Living in a continual realm of peace "by the water streams," Christ could

---

[145] Isa. 11:3, NKJV notes mine

[146] Song of Sol. 5:12, NIV

sleep through any storm. It was out of the realm of victorious inner stillness that He operated.

The Lord's eyes are bathed in the milk. What is this milk? Peter tells us that we are to crave "pure spiritual milk," and so this is the milk of Holy Spirit.[147] But Paul also tells us that milk is the "truths of God's word."[148] This means that Jesus' eyes view everything through Spirit and Truth. Finally, His eyes are mounted like jewels, seeing completely in multiple dimensions – like every facet of a jewel, Christ sees the big picture. His perfect wisdom leaves no room for impartial judgment, faulty conclusions or an unsympathetic priesthood.

+ Sevens of Completion

The study of the sevenfold encompasses a bit of technical and numerical symbology – from the layout of the lampstand to the counting of the almond buds. But it is ultimately a revelation of God's perfect love. It is about the fullness of His Presence and the fire of intimacy burning within us. As it is the Glory of God to conceal a matter, and the Glory of kings to search it out, let us peer briefly into more prophetic *sevens* found throughout the course of scripture. Every *seven* in the universe is a prophetic portrait of the Spirit of God.

Even the name Jesus – *Yeshua* in Hebrew – has seven points resting on the letters, just like the lampstand:

---

[147] See 1 Pet. 2:2

[148] See Heb. 5:12

ישוע

Throughout the Bible, we have noted that seven is always a number of completion or perfection. The "sevenfold" Spirit of God speaks of Holy Spirit in His fullness. Likewise, John sees a vision of seven separate lampstands in the Book of Revelation. This speaks of the entire church walking in fullness – even as each individual congregation within the whole also possesses the fullness of God. Even the individual believer has Christ's perfect wholeness within Him. And paradoxically, we are all interdependent upon one another to express this fullness as a united, corporate whole.

The Book of Revelation speaks of seven angels, seven horns, seven trumpets, seven thunders, seven bowls and seven churches. There are seven days of creation, wherein the seventh is the holy day of completion. Since then, humanity has always observed seven days in the week. In Song of Solomon chapter four, Christ describes seven facets of His bride. He sees her in fullness. Furthermore, there are seven colors of the rainbow given to Noah after the flood. God's covenant with Noah was a prophesy of the coming of His Holy Spirit.

Did you ever consider that the seven colors of the rainbow all stem from pure, invisible white light? Seven colors in one. Man only sees light when it is broken into these seven colors. This represents the visible, tangible, manifest interactions of an otherwise invisible Holy Spirit. These colors are observable when broken down through a prism. These are all natural enigmas – because everything in the physical universe is a shadowy reflection of the invisible God.

Such natural blueprints can be rather precise in their predictions of heavenly realities. Light is broken down into three primary colors, and three secondary colors. The color spectrum further breaks down into *twelve*. Consider the twelve heavenly foundations, or the twelve apostolic pillars of the church – a governmental, ruling number. If you broke the color spectrum down again, it would come to twenty-four colors. Consider the twenty-four elders worshipping around the throne. It is quite likely that Holy Spirit is the very *emerald rainbow around the throne*. Down here, on Earth, we only see in part. But we do not have time to talk about all of these details now.

Furthermore, Heaven is full of eyes. Everything is visible and manifest. There is no hiding or lurking in shadows there. The living creatures have eyes all over themselves. I once had a visionary experience where I encountered a living creature. I was in a meeting, and no one else was aware of what I was seeing. Suddenly, all of the eyes flew off the creature, and landed on someone! It was very startling! I never knew that the living creatures had detachable eyes. You can imagine my amusement. Somehow I knew that this person was receiving a revelatory impartation from the eyes of the living creatures. Granted, this was all very strange. But the Lord reminded me that His own eyes are moveable. *His eyes range to and fro throughout the Earth*.

Did you know that your spiritual eyes are not bound by your natural, physical body? In the Glory realm, your vision is inter-dimensional. Elisha could see into the enemy king's war chambers, and he was able to warn God's people of the adversary's plans. Likewise, you can see what is going on geographically in other places. And you can see what is happening in heavenly dimensions. Jesus' eyes knew the thoughts of men's hearts. In this way, your spiritual eyes can discern hidden things.

The seven Spirits are His moving eyes – and they are *your* moving eyes.

In Ezekiel chapter one, we read of God's mobile throne moving from place to place on *Glory wheels*. These are *wheels within a wheel*, and they are absolutely covered in eyes![149] While there are many interpretations to these passages and their meanings, the scriptures do say that the spirits of the living creatures were *in the wheels*, and they would move wherever Holy Spirit would go. These intersecting wheels do speak of mobility in multiple, intersecting dimensions. Your spiritual sight is quickened by Holy Spirit to see in many planes of reality at once. In the same way that God is omniscient, or *all seeing*, remember that you are made in His image with His blueprints inside of you! You literally have ability – when moved by His Spirit – to be aware of many things simultaneously. There is a very real degree with which you possess God's divine, omniscient nature within you as a new creation in Christ. I do not believe that Adam's brain was limited to ten percent of its function. When man's spirit is moving in unison with God's, we know everything He knows. As the apostle Paul says, *we have the mind of Christ*.[150] Ignorance and spiritual blindness were byproducts of the fall of man-

---

149 See Ezek. 1:16-18

150 See 1 Cor. 2:16

kind. But Christ, the Last Adam, has purchased a new heart for you, opening windows of mind and soul to dimensions beyond what the first Adam possessed.

The seven eyes of the Lamb speak of His omniscient knowing. The seven horns of the Lamb speak of His omnipotent power. Just as you have access to all He knows, so also can you access all that He can do. Not just the vision ... but the authority to make it happen.

+ The Number Seven

Consider briefly some of the numeric correlations in the scriptures, regarding the number seven. St. Augustine said, "Numbers are the universal language offered by the deity to humans as confirmation of the truth."[151] You need not be a mathematician to appreciate the appearance of God in statistics. While the Christian does not approach numbers the way a magician or numerologist would, they can provide powerful prophetic approvals to scripture.

"The number seven is good, but we do not explain it after the doctrine of Pythagoras and the other philosophers, but rather according to the manifestation and division of the grace of the Spirit; for the prophet Isaias has enumerated the principal gifts of the Holy Spirit as seven," writes St. Ambrose.[152] A number of early church fathers appealed to numbers in their interpreta-

---

[151] "Numerology," *Wikipedia, The Free Encyclopedia*, http://en.wikipedia.org/wiki/Numerology (accessed July 15, 2009).
[152] "Numerology and the Church Fathers," *Wikipedia, The Free Encyclopedia*, http://en.wikipedia.org/wiki/Numerology_and_the_Church_Fathers (accessed July 10, 2010).

tive work, while always cautioning us against pushing their mystical symbolism to the extreme.

God created the world in seven days. The number has always divided time for cultures around the world. We know that Enoch was the seventh from Adam – among other things, he was prophetic of a people who would walk again with God after Adam's fall. The Lord overthrew seven nations in Canaan to give the land as an inheritance. And there were seven deacons appointed to the church in Acts 6. Noah entered the ark with seven others, waiting seven days before the flood to begin, and even the animals entered by sevens. There were seven days that lapsed between the two missions of the dove (a symbol of the Spirit). After the flood in his day, the waters of the Earth formed seven seas – prophetic of Holy Spirit hovering over its waters at the dawn of creation.

There are seven pillars in wisdom's house,[153] and seven locks in Samson's hair, who was consecrated to God in the Spirit of Might.[154] Jesus is the Root and Branch of Jesse, who was the father of seven sons. There are twice seven generations in the lineage of Jesus.[155]

Naaman dipped in the river seven times for His healing – a foreshadow of Spirit baptism for the Gentiles who would believe Christ.[156] Jacob worked for Leah and then Rachel for seven years each.[157] Marriage festivals

---

153 See Prov. 9:1

154 See Judg. 16:13, 19

155 See Matt. 1:17

156 See 2 Kings 5

157 See Gen. 29

lasted seven days.[158] The Israelites marched around Jericho seven times for its defeat – speaking of our complete authority in Christ and absolute breakthrough for those who walk in the Spirit, rather than their own might.[159] On the seventh day, they walked around the city seven times, while seven priests blew seven horns. Seven days were given as a period of ceremonial cleansing for various impurities and diseases. It was also the time period prescribed for Aaron and his sons for priestly ordination, when the blood and the oil were applied to them.[160] Did you know that you have been given a sevenfold ordination?

In various Levitical ceremonies, blood is sprinkled seven times before the Lord.

Jesus broke seven loaves – symbolic of Himself – and multiplied them to the masses. There were seven baskets left over – as there is more than enough of Him for the nations.[161]

While we will go to great lengths in elaborating on the Spirit's sevenfold nature, please remember an overarching principle. We must not be too literal or exacting with our description of God's operations. This is *God Himself* of which we speak! By no means is He limited to seven linear dynamics or functions. For the most part, remember that the term "seven" is used parabolically to describe His wholeness or fullness.

---

[158] See Gen. 29:27

[159] See Josh. 5, 6

[160] See Lev. 8:33

[161] See Mark 8

"Seven was a sacred number in the Jewish church: but it did not always imply a precise number. It sometimes is to be taken figuratively, to denote completeness or perfection," wrote John Wesley.[162]

For instance, in the Earth at large, seven "was also a sacred number among the Hebrews and other Semites, and also among Aryans of Persia and even of Greece. Its sacredness is traceable to remote antiquity."[163] This sacred element attached to the number contributes to its use in a trans-literary manner.

"The frequent recurrence of certain numbers in the sacred literature of the Hebrews ... in some instances to lose their numerical force, and to pass over into the province of symbolic signs," states *Smith's Dictionary of the Bible*. "But (the number) seven so far surpasses the rest ... it may fairly be termed the *representative* symbolic number."[164]

+ PENTECOST: THE FEAST OF SEVENS

The number seven is replete in the Book of Revelation. Writes expositor William Mounce, "In this apocalyptic genre, the number seven is normally infused with symbolic value."[165] Seven times, John says, "He who has an

---

[162] Wesley, *John Wesley's Notes on the Whole Bible: The New Testament*, Notes on The Revelation of John.

[163] John Davis and Henry Gehman, ed., *The Westminster Dictionary of the Bible* (Philadelphia: The Westminster Press, 1898), 546.

[164] H.B. Hackett, *Smith's Dictionary of the Bible*, Vol. IV (Grand Rapids: Baker Book House, 1870), 2934.

[165] William D. Mounce, *Mounce's Complete Expository Dictionary of Old & New Testament Words* (Grand Rapids: Zondervan, 2006), 638.

ear, let him hear what *the Spirit* says to the Churches."[166] *Seven* is used fifty-four times in the Revelation, and *seventh* is used five times. Nine of these cases refer to demonic or otherwise "wicked" sevens. Subtract those, and you have a total of fifty *sevens* used in reference to holy things. This is far more significant than one may realize.

The number fifty is very important prophetic number in the study of Holy Spirit. We know that it is the number of *Jubilee.* The Israelites were commanded to let the land rest every seven years – this was a *Sabbath year.* They were to allow their fields to lie fallow and do no farming work for an entire year. This required trust – as *rest* always does – because God said He would always bring a supernatural increase on the sixth year, abundantly providing enough food for everyone to take the seventh year off. How would you like to coast on a free ride every seventh year? This is where we get our modern concept of a *sabbatical.*

After seven of these seven-year cycles, or forty nine years, the Israelites were to take yet another year off! This fiftieth year was the year of Jubilee. Interestingly, the scriptures also tell us that the Levites were also supposed to *retire* at age fifty – it is a number symbolic of rest. It represented the completed work of the priest – the finished work of Christ.

God would provide enough grain and crops in the fields on the forty-eighth year, so that the entire nation could take off work for *two years*! This included their ordinary Sabbath year, plus the additional year of Jubilee.

---

[166] See Rev. 2:7, 11, 17, 29; Rev. 3:6, 13, 22

The Jubilee was something that every generation would have an opportunity to experience, at least once in their lifetime.

Not only did people rest, but on Jubilee, there was a requirement for all debts to be cancelled. Furthermore, all slaves had to be released on this year! The entire economy was reset in the year of Jubilee. It was a time of liberty. However, the Israelites failed horribly to observe the Jubilee as they should.

One of the main reasons the Israelites were brought into the Babylonian captivity for seventy years was because they failed to observe their Sabbath years. They spent one year in captivity for every Sabbath that they missed. They had not recognized the Jubilee either.[167] God is serious about rest. He's serious about having fun! He is serious about us trusting Him. When we neglect rest, we may think we are being noble by working harder and *getting ahead* in life. But forfeiture of rest is indicative of pride. Self-reliance versus trusting God. The Lord has a brilliant way of causing all that extra labor to send us backward, instead of ahead. Men, who toil an eighty-hour workweek, always neglecting rest, will surely lose the very thing they sweat for – through calamity and setbacks. Never think that increase comes from the arm of flesh. But God increases those He favors.

Learning about Jubilee helps us to understand *Pentecost* – the feast we most associate with the first outpouring of Holy Spirit. It also helps us to unlock some mysteries in the Book of Revelation.

---

[167] See Lev. 26:23-24, 32-35, 43

Pentecost is the Jewish Feast of Weeks – or more appropriately, the *Feast of Sevens*. In Hebrew, *shabuwa* means both *week* and *seven.*[168] Pentecost was a feast of first fruits that occurred every year, following seven cycles of seven days – or forty-nine days. The fiftieth day was Pentecost.
Are you seeing the theme of seven sevens, followed by a celebratory number fifty?

We will look more into Pentecost later. But for now, let us just tie a few of these numbers together. You might be amazed at how simple this becomes.

John sees seven, separate lampstands in Revelation – each of these menorah is burning with its own seven lamps. This makes a total of forty-nine flames burning. And there, in the midst of the forty-nine flames was *One who walks among the seven golden lampstands!*[169] All of the lamps point to Jesus. Christ is the number fifty among the seven churches. All of the forty-nine days in the Feast of Weeks point to Him – *He is the day of Pentecost.* All of the forty-nine years of Sabbath cycles point to our ultimate, eternal Sabbath which is Christ – *He is the year of Jubilee*! It is in Christ that we find rest, in Christ that our debts are cancelled, and in Christ that our yoke of slavery is removed.

The Day of Pentecost was about Christ coming to walk among His church. Seven cycles of seven always point to a climatic conclusion in Christ. In Heaven, they always shine upon Him.

---

[168] Strong, *Exhaustive Concordance of the Bible*, Entry 7620.
[169] See Rev. 2:1

+ SOLOMON'S LAMPSTANDS

Until now, we have seen the lampstand as a singular object in the Tabernacle of Moses. We have also seen a heavenly picture of not one, but seven lampstands in the Book of Revelation. There remains one more archetype we have not yet explored.

In Solomon's Temple, the king ordered that ten lampstands be constructed. Departing from the Mosaic model of only *one* lampstand, this tenfold model required a total of seventy lamps of fire resting on ten menorahs. Again, they all pointed to the table of shewbread – but why the introduction of ten candlesticks?

We know that to the Jews, the number ten finds its chief significance in the Ten Commandments – considered by far to be the holiest part of the Torah. The law could not truly be fulfilled but through Christ, bringing a penultimate fulfillment in the church, who would become living epistles. But these ten stands carried seven flames each. The number seventy is of particular interest in the study of scriptures. For one, it represents the nations of the Earth. In Genesis 10, we see a precise listing of seventy nations coming from the lineage of Noah. Subsequently, these are the nations that immediately set to work on the tower of Babel in Genesis 11, before God scattered them and divided their languages.

When Holy Spirit was poured out on Pentecost, we read that "there were staying in Jerusalem God-fearing Jews from every nation under heaven" and that each heard the disciples speaking in their own language.[170] As the language of the Spirit was released on Pentecost, God reversed the curse of Babel to the redeemed of the Earth. Only in the Spirit can we have true unity as a royal nation. On Pentecost, the Spirit was poured out on all flesh to all the nations of the Earth.

Seventy bulls were sacrificed each year at the Feast of Tabernacles, as this prophetically indicated Christ's atoning sacrifice for all the nations of the Earth.[171] And in Solomon's day, Israel was in its *golden period* of sorts. It was truly the most prosperous nation of the Earth, and bore more influence and stature in world affairs than ever before or since. God was showcasing His chosen before the peoples of the Earth for His Glory. He loves to make us *famous for our bliss*![172] It is no wonder that the seventy lamps would have burned in Solomon's era.

When Jesus sent His seventy disciples out to preach the good news of the Kingdom, it represented a divine commissioning that would go to all nations. Of course, He had not yet died on the cross, so these seventy only ministered within Israel. The way had not been opened to the gentiles. But it was the *number* of them that was most prophetic – showing that the good news would eventually go to every tribe and tongue. We do not read that the seventy were Levites – nor was Christ – for this would be a priesthood of *all believers*, not a certain class born by natural lineage.

---

170 Acts 2:5, NIV

171 See Num. 29

172 Gen. 12:2, MOF

The other example of this number most prominent in scripture occurs in the story of the seventy elders who were simultaneously taken into a heavenly encounter with Moses on the mountain.[173] This was an exotic corporate encounter, often forgotten or overlooked by scholars. For instance, the ground was paved with sapphires and they all ate a meal with God. These men represented a counsel of all nationalities that would one day be included in a New Covenant, as the seventy were literally the "heads of households." They represented the entire populace, not just Moses or Aaron. Again we see these seventy elders corporately endowed with the spirit of prophesy in Numbers 11.

Scholars point to a "scribal error" in Luke 10, as some ancient manuscripts say that Jesus sent *seventy* disciples out, while other versions say He commissioned *seventy-two* disciples. I do not believe in *scribal errors* of this nature. I believe scripture is infallible. Such claims only spark my attention, and cause me to dig for mysteries. I always believe there are reasons for these ancient variants in text. So were there seventy or seventy-two? When studying this matter, I returned to the example of the seventy elders prophesying with Moses in Numbers 11, and I found the following passage. While Moses and the seventy were receiving a prophetic impartation from the Lord, this is what occurred simultaneously in the camp of the Jews:

> *However,* ***two men****, whose names were Eldad and Medad, had remained in the camp. They were listed among the elders, but did not go out to the Tent* (with the other seventy). *Yet the Spirit also rested*

---

[173] See Exod. 24

on them, and they prophesied in the camp. A young man ran and told Moses, "Eldad and Medad are prophesying in the camp."

Joshua son of Nun, who had been Moses' aide since youth, spoke up and said, "Moses, my lord, stop them!"

But Moses replied, "Are you jealous for my sake? I wish that all the Lord's people were prophets and that the Lord would put His Spirit on them!"[174]

And so, we read here that Moses imparted the Spirit to seventy elders, but it even spilled over to the two extra stragglers in the camp! It is amazing to consider the layered depths of scripture! The seventy and the seventy-two are somehow the same. And this seemingly minor and obscure differentiation was even predicted in the far more ancient Hebrew text of Numbers. Do the extra two hint at the two olive trees? The two witnesses in the camp? Quite possibly. We know that in Solomon's temple, we see a blueprint of all the nations of the Earth burning with the Glory of God.

+ THE SEVEN STARS

By delving into much symbolic detail, my desire is not to distract the reader from the main points. Rather, I only hope to stabilize and unpack our primary themes. You are a lampstand, flowing with a sevenfold river of oil. It is the oil of His Presence, the oil of His grace. And within even the simplest of believers dwells the headwaters of eternal Rivers of Life.

---

[174] Num. 11:26-29, NIV notes mine

This sevenfold torrent, like the oil flowing through Zechariah's lampstand, is limitless and eternally flowing through you. Perhaps the light of revelation has not yet touched the flame to your branches. Perhaps you don't know what is inside of you – but know that God Himself has completely taken residence within.

It is not the angels but the oil of His sevenfold Spirit that flows through you continuously. Wisdom is not an angel. Paul says that *Christ is the Wisdom of God.* Power is not an angel. Paul tells us in the same verse that *Christ is the Power of God.*[175] In fact, all of the seven Spirits of God are Christ's Spirits, not angels. Consider it this way:

Christ is the Lord
Christ is Wisdom
Christ is Understanding
Christ is Counsel
Christ is Mighty Power
Christ is the Knowledge of God
Christ is the Fear of the Lord

But here, we should receive a bit of understanding. *For there are angels who minister the seven Spirits.* God does indeed use angels to do His bidding, and those angels are sent to minister and serve the heirs of salvation.

> *Praise the Lord, you His angels, you mighty ones who do His bidding, who obey His word.*[176]

---

[175] See 1 Cor. 1:24

[176] Ps. 103:20, NIV

CHAPTER THREE

Are not all angels ministering spirits sent to serve those who will inherit salvation?[177]

Angels are those who *execute* God's orders. In fact, God rarely does anything except that He outsources His tasks to the angels. And often, those angels are going about tasks that help and benefit us.

Jesus mentions seven angels – calling them *seven stars* – along with the churches in Revelation 1, who are "the angels of the seven churches." The messages Christ sends to the seven churches are actually addressed to the angels themselves, (i.e. *to the angel of the church at Ephesus write.* ...). It is clear that these angels are messengers to the churches (again, "angel" means *messenger*), but their assignments are more comprehensive. Angels are not limited to the roles of simply blowing horns and delivering scrolls. They are not mere cupids or guardian angels. In fact, we don't really see guardian angels in scripture, except perhaps to guard the Tree of Life. It is a bit trite to truncate their assignment as strictly defensive or protective in nature. Clearly they do offer protection, as "He shall give His angels charge over you, to keep you in all your ways."[178] But guardianship is not necessarily their primary role. The closest scriptural example of a "guardian" angel would be found in Ezekiel's prophecy to the king of Tyre, calling him the "cherub that covereth" or "guardian cherub."[179] But many scholars consider this allegorical of the pre-fallen satan. You don't want satan as your guardian angel!

---

[177] Heb. 1:14, NIV

[178] See Ps. 91:11

[179] See Ezek. 28:14-16

Among their many and assorted roles – from healing to warfare – angels carry vastly important assignments. My wife once met an angel named Sovereignty. Did it somehow minister an aspect of the sovereignty of the Lord? It showed her things that came to pass in God's sovereign plan. Angels carry weighty assignments. We do know angelic regents can hold sway over regions, people groups, individuals and far more in scriptures. God uses angels to minister different aspect of His own character, virtues, miraculous abilities and more. In John 5, we see a healing angel stirring the waters of Bethesda. In the Book of Acts, Peter was released from prison by a *deliverance* angel. There are many assignments and roles they have. Some attend to worship and the arts. Not all minister what we would deem "spiritual" gifts, such as prophecy, etc. – although all their work is spiritual. There are angels that execute Kingdom work in our finances, those assigned over earthly governments, as well as those assigned to bizarre miracles such as multiplication of food, walking through walls or floating right off the ground. Angels are involved in just about everything. Of course, we do not worship angels, but scripture is full of conversations with angels. Many religious streams have such a paranoia regarding the ministry of angels; they would rather ignore it or suppress it. They think any talk of angels flirts with the possibility of us worshipping them. I think Christians today are more prone to worship movie stars than angels. Our problem today is not a propensity toward worshipping them, as much as a propensity toward not believing they exist.

If we ignore the participation of angels, or vainly assume we don't need their interaction, then we have allowed fear and pride to cut us off from a wealth of power and fruitfulness. This is not to say that we must have a conscious awareness of their work among us at all times. But I want to always have enough humility to receive God's help in my life and ministry, whether it comes from an angel, a person or Balaam's ass.

With this in mind, I believe that the *seven stars* are a special class of angels assigned most specifically toward the ministry, or functioning of God's own sevenfold Spirit. They are also associated with the seven churches, which are parabolic of the church universal.

What I am about to share in the next few paragraphs is personal opinion, and beliefs on such matters should remain such. There are a few deluded folks out there who have framed entire rigid theologies on the sevenfold based on their own ideas and their personal subjective visions. They say that anyone who is not "personally tutored" by these seven elusive cosmic beings cannot speak rightly about the sevenfold. Don't be intimidated by such spiritual elitism, nor be beguiled away from the simplicity of Christ. The scriptures must be our authoritative, final word on matters of question.

I believe these *seven stars* could be angelic beings of the highest caliber. They are not mere messengers in the sense of delivering prophetic words. These seven represent something *more*. Their association with the sevenfold Spirit of God appears to denote a direct role in appropriating and ministering these seven virtues of Holy Spirit to the church. I believe the angels assist in the function and operation of the seven streams of God, which they act as corporate stewards or *releasers*.

It is not overtly clear from scripture that there are angels specifically assigned to the sevenfold. But there could be an angel of wisdom and an angel of understanding – just as there are angels of counsel, might, knowledge and the fear of the Lord. In fact, there is even an Angel of the Lord. The *Angel of the Lord*, often thought to be Christ represented in the Old Testament, could possibly be the *center pipe* angel as it were. Though this is quite likely Christ Himself in some form in the Old Testament – the only angel who commanded and accepted worship. We must remember that the word "angel" simply means *messenger.* And Christ is truly the chief Messenger of the Father.

Even the ancient Jews spoke of seven angels of the presence. There is a long-held, traditional viewpoint held by the liturgical church that *seven archangels* hold sway over the highest affairs of God. There surely seems to be lots of evidence to assume this is so, but most of that evidence is apocryphal. One such resource for understanding the interaction of angels is the Book of Enoch. While Enoch is not included in our canon of scripture, most scholars hold that it is of *some* value. However, like any apocryphal book, we do not hold it as *infallible* (absolutely perfect). There are clearly fanciful parts of Enoch that are not true – for instance, nine-hundred-foot giants roaming the land seems a bit much. While we know giants existed, Biblical references put them quite a bit shorter than that. This is one of many discrepancies in Enoch. Select parts and volumes are beneficial as an ancillary help to our studies. Don't make Enoch your primary diet or focus on it too much.

The thing about Enoch that differentiates it from most other apocryphal books is that Jude actually quotes from Enoch directly in his own New Testament epistle. If Jude uses it, then it seems reasonable that we can glean a few things from it as well. Unlike the false gnostic gospels (Thomas, Judas, Mary, etc.), which are popularized by the Da Vinci Code and are blatantly heretical – we must make a clear differentiation between helpful apocryphal literature and the bad stuff. I do not recommend the Book of Adam and Eve, the Book of Giants or many of these other more whimsical volumes.

Enoch speaks of "the seven first white ones."[180] And in other passages, names seven chief watcher angels:

> *And these are the names of the holy angels who watch. Uriel, one of the holy angels, who is over the world and over Tartarus. Raphael, one of the holy angels, who is over the spirits of men. Raguel, one of the holy angels who takes vengeance on the world of the luminaries. Michael, one of the holy angels, to wit, he that is set over the best part of mankind and over chaos. Saraqâêl, one of the holy angels, who is set over the spirits, who sin in the spirit. Gabriel, one of the holy angels, who is over Paradise and the serpents and the Cherubim. Remiel, one of the holy angels, whom God set over those who rise.*[181]

I have no personal propensity to *believe* in these named angels above. I only include this passage for educational purposes, to relay the long-standing concept of

---

[180] See 1 En. 90:21

[181] 1 En. 20:1-8

seven archangels. Names and details have a high likelihood of being spurious.

Another apocryphal book that is highly regarded in the Catholic and Orthodox church, and is considered deuterocanonical (part of the second canon) is the *Book of Tobit*. It was removed from the Jewish canon in late antiquity, as well as from the Protestant Bible in the seventeenth century. Tobit makes further reference to angels. Besides Michael and Gabriel there are no other explicitly *named* angels in the Bible. However, Tobit names one more – Raphael – which is perhaps the most solid, widely accepted reference to a named angel outside of scripture. In Tobit's encounter with Raphael, the angel mentions a special crew of seven angelic majesties.

> *For I am the angel Raphael, one of the seven, who stand before the Lord.*[182]

Are these seven the same as the seven stars? The same as the seven who blow the trumpets and release judgments in the Book of Revelation? It is difficult to discern when considering non-canonical figures. However, there may be some truth and benefit to investigate, and it is worth study, rather than skepticism in these matters. Raphael's words are a striking resemblance to those of Gabriel:

> *I am Gabriel. I stand in the presence of God. ...*[183]

---

182 Tob. 12:15

183 Luke 1:19, NIV

And furthermore, there is similarity to the following passage:

> *And I saw the seven angels who stand before God, and to them were given seven trumpets.*[184]

First century Rabbi Pirkey Eliezer speaks of "the angels which were first created minister before Him without the veil," and Jewish tradition holds to "seven cohorts or troops of angels, under whom are thirty inferior orders."[185]

The problem with angelology, or the study of angels, is that there are too many conflicting writings regarding names and roles of specific angels. Perhaps the most explanatory source of apocryphal writings on this matter is Enoch. But Enoch is actually composed of different volumes, likely written hundreds of years apart by numerous authors. It is spurious, of highly questionable authenticity, and should not be canonical just because Jude, a canonical writer, quoted it. Paul himself quoted secular writers, but that doesn't mean they should be canonized.

There is balance needed. The church has always viewed apocryphal books to be *of some value*. It is only a recent concept that all apocryphal books are somehow bad. The Catholic church recognizes Gabriel, Michael and Raphael; the Orthodox church recognizes a few others, including Uriel. In an Eastern Orthodox feast, Uriel is commemorated together with the other archangels in

---

184 Rev. 8:2, NKJV

185 Adam Clarke, *Commentary on the Whole Bible* (Eight Volumes, 1810-1826. Available online at http://www.godrules.net. Excerpt from Revelation 1.

the "Synaxis of the Archangel Michael and the Other Bodiless Powers." Interestingly, even Anglican and Episcopalian Protestants officially recognize the angel Uriel.

Another apocryphal book – the Second Book of Esdras – also mentions the name Uriel, an angel highlighted extensively by Enoch. The writer of Second Esdras mentions nine angels who will rule at the end of the world, five of which are not mentioned in any other apocryphal work. Furthermore, there are a plethora of modern charismatic leaders and historical saints who have interacted with specifically named angels, both today and in church history. We should not be skeptical of the validity unless it distracts from the person of Christ, puts undue attention on the minister or is overtly unbiblical or misleading. We should never dismiss such encounters, but also recognize that these are all subjective experiences at the end of the day. *I love subjective experiences!* I see angels quite regularly. But the bottom line is that we do not base a theology on them.

It is unusual for a Christian *not* to encounter angels as a normative experience. From my studies, I believe this was a standard way of life in the early church. From my experience, I know that we do not wait for angels to come into our realm. We have open access into theirs.

There is clearly an Angel of the Lord. And there are angels who minister God's wisdom, understanding, counsel, might, knowledge and the fear of the Lord. These are conjoined to the work of the sevenfold Spirit of God. Much of their nature remains a mystery if we are confined merely to the text. But these very angels are at our disposal as servants and messengers to the church. They enable us, sustain us and equip us via the agency of Holy Spirit Himself.

What we can know for certain is that these seven stars are the angels of the seven churches.[186] And their messages correlate to that which the Lord spoke to Ephesus, Smyrna, Pergamum, Thyatira, Sardis, Philadelphia and Laodecia. The messengers are not our focus, but rather the message.

In the next three chapters, we will begin to explore the specific dynamics of the seven Spirits of God Himself. We have already discussed the center pipe of the lampstand – the *Spirit of the Lord.* This is the most exclusive of the seven branches, because it tells us *who He is*. It is the firm and non-negotiable standard of our faith. We are saved by Christ alone. It is His name above all names by which we are grafted into the Vine, and out of which all else flows. In the subsequent chapters, we will look now at the other six operations of His nature: *Wisdom, Understanding, Counsel, Power, Knowledge* and the *Fear of the Lord.*

---

186 See Rev. 1:20

+ Chapter Four
Wisdom & Understanding

It is amazing how the Lord has brought a restoration of the spiritual gifts to the church through the Pentecostal and charismatic movements of the past century. But the seven Spirits of God are light years beyond a mere *spiritual gift*. We are talking about the gift-giver Himself.

It is one thing to possess the gift called a *word of wisdom*. It is another thing to *become possessed* by the Spirit of Wisdom. The word of wisdom is merely a by-product fellowship with the Spirit of Wisdom; likewise, words of knowledge come from the Spirit of Knowledge. The words are gifts; the Spirit is a person.

> *For to one is given the word of wisdom through the Spirit, to another the word of knowledge through the same Spirit.*[187]

These gifts – individual words from God – are meager crumbs compared to the eternal river of Wisdom Itself. You can be continually plugged in to the very wisdom of Holy Spirit at all times. This is unlike a singular bit of information that you may receive in an occasional prayer time. Rather, it is a constant flow of wisdom at all times in the life of a believer.

Wisdom is an anointing from God. It is tangible and can be imparted. It is a *Spirit*. It is literally a *divine ability* or supernatural enabling for learning, doing, building and receiving great favor. True wisdom is not an esoteric intellectualism. It is not theology or philoso-

---

[187] 1 Cor. 12:8, NKJV

phy. Neither is it a gnostic form of "saving" wisdom that rejects the work of the cross. Simply stated, wisdom is *revelatory* in nature. It is God revealed to us. And how can we love God more, unless He is displayed to us in a greater way?

> *I keep asking that the God of our Lord Jesus Christ, the glorious Father, may give you the Spirit of wisdom and revelation, so that you may know Him better.*[188]

If in some way, wisdom represents the mind of God, then it is ever speaking about the heart of God. Love is the fulfillment of true wisdom.

+ Lessons From a Sadhu

One man in church history particularly exemplifies a life operated out of the Spirit of Wisdom. His name is Sadhu Sundar Singh. Sundar was an Indian Christian minister at the dawn of the twentieth century. His life was chock full of supernatural happenings – foremost of which were his continual, one-on-one encounters with Jesus Christ. Singh experienced regular, face-to-face conversations with the Lord, which are documented extensively in several of his books. His was an abiding habitation in the Glory realm.

You are in a continual face-to-face encounter with the Lord right now, but perhaps you are unaware of it!

I have briefly documented the life of Sundar in one of my previous books, *The New Mystics*. But his life is

---

[188] Eph. 1:17, NIV

particularly relevant as we discuss the Spirit of Wisdom. Sundar lived out of the cloud of wisdom. He was born to an upper class Sikh family, and from the age of five, he was trained to pray for hours a day. He was zealous for his faith, and was accustomed to persecuting Christian missionaries. He even burned a Bible in defiance of Christianity. His life's goal was to become an Indian holy man, living a life of poverty and prayer. By the age of fourteen, Jesus Christ supernaturally revealed Himself to Sundar in a brilliant vision of light. Sundar was radically converted, and his family immediately disowned him for his new faith. They booted him from the house, instantly dropping him from the top of the caste system down to abject poverty. His own kin even poisoned his last meal in an attempt to kill him.

Sundar maintained the deeply instilled discipline of hours of daily meditation – but now he knew to whom he was praying. Sundar began to have visions, Heavenly translations and exotic angelic encounters. Angelic agents often rescued him from perilous situations and persecutions. On one of his missionary journeys, a hostile group, opposed to the gospel, dropped him into a well that was full of human bones. He was left for dead. An unknown figure freed him from the pit, unlocking him late at night. The next day, Sundar was seen boldly preaching again on the same streets. The village leader was terrified at the miraculous escape, because only he possessed the key to the locked well, which was still tied around his own neck, underneath his robe! Sundar's stories are phenomenal, as he was persecuted often – sometimes in almost preposterous James Bond scenarios. For instance, he was once tied up in a wet yak skin, which was left to dry up and crush him to death! Or tied up and left to be eaten by wild animals. In one of his most controversial experiences, Sundar reported meeting a four-hundred-year-old Christian hermit in the mountains of Tibet. Although this sounds far fetched, we have discussed the supernatural phenomena of extended longevity in my other books.

Sundar lived between Heaven and Earth. Frequent ecstasies and trances were the regular fare for him, and often He met with the Lord Himself in open visitations, where he asked questions and received answers. Besides meditating on the scriptures for hours, and sometimes all day and night, Sundar would spend much time in silent prayer and prayers of recollection. He was deeply contemplative, and his contemporaries regularly struggled to pull him out of deep ecstasies – sometimes he would be missing when it was time for him to preach. They would find him dazed out, sitting in a corner of the room with a big grin on his face! Throughout his life, Sundar wrote a number of books, including detailed documentations of Heavenly visitations.

In one encounter, satan approached Sundar and offered him millions of followers if Sundar would only bow down and worship him. When Sundar realized what was happening, he rebuked the devil. As soon as he did this, Sundar turned his head to see Jesus standing on his other side, face to face. The Lord told Sundar that he was well pleasing in His sight, and to ask what he wanted and he would receive it. All that Sundar wanted was to sit at the Master's feet and have one-on-one conversations with the Lord in the place of intimacy. From that point forward, Sundar's life seemed to be one constant stream of questions and answers with the Lord, which he documented and preserved for us in many of his books and teachings.

Sundar mysteriously disappeared in 1929. His body was never found, and many speculated that he went to live with the old hermit, or perhaps took his place. The Lord once told Sundar that many people had been translated straight into Heaven – and that Elijah and Enoch were not the only ones to ever have such an experience.[189]

Wisdom does come in less bizarre packages. When we consider those who carried a true mantle of wisdom, we may think of C.S. Lewis – or perhaps more modern examples of prophetic teachers such as Rick Joyner or Bill Johnson. But ultimately, Christ is our model of perfect wisdom.

+ CHRIST OUR WISDOM

The apostle Paul was firmly established in the scriptures. As he wrote his epistles, truly he had a revelation of the ancient wisdom literature. He knew from Proverbs, Ecclesiastes and other scriptures that wisdom was *personified* in the sacred text.

Paul must have been intimately familiar with the Book of Proverbs, which tells us that wisdom dwelt with God in the beginning, partnering together in the creation of the world. It was present from before the world began, when the heavens were set in place and the horizon was marked out on the face of the deep. Proverbs 8 also states that wisdom was "given birth," but never that it

---

189 A valuable source on the life of Sundar Singh is *The Saffron Robe* by Janet Lynn Watson (London: Hodder and Stoughton, 1975).

was "created." Paul extensively grasped the Messianic nature of these Jewish texts. And for this reason, he said of the incarnate Christ that He "has become for us wisdom from God."[190]

Jesus grew in wisdom as a man does. Yet He did not merely possess it as a man does. He is Wisdom. Again, Paul says Christ is "the power of God and the wisdom of God."[191]

> *I (Wisdom) love those who love me, and those who seek me find me.*[192]

Wisdom is more than an accumulation of facts and knowledge. It transcends learning and the intellect. He is the living substance of God who must captivate our hearts.

+ SOPHIA

Wisdom, or *sophia* in the Greek, is always used in the feminine gender. There are all manner of bizzaro beliefs and new age conjecture around this fact. But where aberrant ideas have sought to perverted scripture, it is critical that the church understand the truth. Wisdom is not a separate being outside of the Godhead. Not an angel or a goddess. The church has erred in regard to this throughout history, believing on one extreme that Sophia speaks of Mary, the mother of Jesus, and on the other extreme, that scripture only allegorizes wisdom's personification as a tangible "being."

---

190 See 1 Cor. 1:30
191 See 1 Cor. 1:24
192 See Prov. 8:17

As for the gender issue, we should not get hung up on that. But it is important to understand that God is neither male nor female. It takes man and woman together to reflect God's image, as we see in the creation account:

> *Then God said, 'Let us make man in our image, in our likeness, and let* ***them*** *rule over the fish of the sea and the birds of the air. ... So God created man in His own image, in the image of God He created him;* ***male and female*** *He created them.*[193]

It is good to remember that we reflect God's image, not the other way around. I believe that most specifically within the Godhead, Holy Spirit reflects those more feminine qualities of God's nature. His sensitivity. His nurture. I do not want to sound chauvinistic, but Holy Spirit is the *Comforter*, the *Helper*. This in no way diminishes His raw power and dominance. This is something that transcends sexuality, but refers to female *personality* traits. God's presence is tender thing of beauty and romance.

+ Resting in Us

Our relationship with Holy Spirit, in this regard, requires a special sensitivity and emotive response that we may not always directly associate with an earthly father image. There is a most holy tenderness and nearness that we experience with Holy Spirit (He dwells within our very being!) that is unique and sacrosanct. Could this deep sensitivity be one of the very reasons

---

[193] Gen. 1:26-27, NIV

we are most cautioned beyond all else against blaspheming Holy Spirit?[194]

Holy Spirit seeks a place to rest, and in this way, we become the very resting place, the very temple of God. We have read of Jesus in Isaiah 11 that, *"the Spirit of the Lord will **rest** on Him;"* likewise *"Wisdom **reposes** (rests) in the heart of the discerning. ..."*[195]

It is the very seal of Holy Spirit upon us and within us that makes us so beautiful to the Bridegroom. The depths of Holy Spirit within us cry out to the depths of Jesus. It is His presence within us that literally draws God to us and us to God. Deep calls out to deep.

Wisdom not only seeks to rest within us, but the Spirit of Wisdom also brings rests to our own souls:

> *Her ways are pleasant ways, and all her paths are peace.*[196]

The yoke of the Lord is light; it is not burdensome. We also read that the anointing, the manifestation of His presence, is the very thing that breaks a heavy yoke. As Christians, we are always living a paradox between working diligently and living lives of rest. There are always two pitfalls to this path: strife and complacency, either of which we can fall into.

But the narrow path is always to align ourselves in a place of rest and submission, so that the Spirit of God is

---

[194] See Mark 3:28-29

[195] Prov. 14:33, NIV

[196] Prov. 3:17, NIV

the One working mightily from within us. Otherwise, we are prone to Saulish labors, sacrificing for God inappropriately with sinful motives. Or like Uzzah, we try to reach out our own hand to uphold the Glory of God. But an arm of flesh cannot uphold God. As we operate out of stillness, we cultivate the interior life. This takes wisdom. To cease from our own labors – even and especially religious ones – God can begin to perform His.

This does not mean we are called to slumber, but it does mean we are not called to toil. Toil – striving labor by the sweat of our brow – is a result of the fall of man and its subsequent curse. But the blood of Christ has freed us from that curse, and He is calling us back into a lifestyle of "garden works," which elicit peace, joy and creativity. The life of faith is one that turns from the toiling anxieties and worries of the world. The world always fends for itself, yet we cheerfully surrender self to God. This, of course, is the wisdom of God that is foolishness to the world.

+ The Oil of Wisdom

There is an *oil of wisdom* – a spiritual anointing from above that is always accompanied by heavenly and even earthly treasures.

> *There is desirable treasure, and oil in the dwelling of the wise, but a foolish man squanders it.*[197]

There are countless benefits and promises toward those who seek, pursue and possess wisdom. God favors those who have wisdom. One moment of favor is worth

[197] See Prov. 21:20

more than a lifetime of self-effort and strife. *"For whoever finds me finds life and receives favor from the Lord."*[198] Possessing wisdom is one of the chief ways of receiving special benefit from God. Consider Solomon, who chose wisdom over wealth and authority. He was given all of the above. Wisdom is a means of avoiding much unnecessary suffering.

When you are anointed with the oil of wisdom, there are many practical benefits you receive. You are supernaturally empowered, for *a wise man has great power.*[199] Wisdom will be *sweet to your soul*, and it brings an irrevocable *future hope* for you that will not be cut off.[200] Lovers of wisdom "inherit wealth, that I may fill their treasuries."[201] They also gain long life, "for by Me your days will be multiplied, and years will be added to your life."[202]

With promises of longer life and more money in the bank, one would think the world would be desperate for wisdom. Words of wisdom alone "will prolong your life many years and bring you prosperity. ... Then you will win favor and a good name in the sight of God and man. ... This will bring health to your body and nourishment to your bones."[203] Words of wisdom are abundant, and they are *life to those who find them, and health to all their flesh.*[204]

---

[198] Prov. 8:35, NIV
[199] See Prov. 24:5
[200] See Prov. 24:14
[201] Prov. 8:21, NKJV
[202] Prov. 9:11, ESV
[203] Prov. 3:2,4,8, NIV
[204] See Prov. 4:22

Although she cries out in the streets, many foolishly turn aside from her ... following their own self-reliant ways. Wisdom literature is replete with promises of extended life, health and financial blessing, as well as peace, enjoyment and security even in this life.

> *Long life is in her right hand; in her left hand are riches and honor.*[205]

> *My son, pay attention to what I say; listen closely to My words ... for they are life to those who find them and health to a man's whole body.*[206]

+ Benefits of Wisdom

There are natural and spiritual benefits of wisdom, that range from the sublime to the very practical abilities for various manner of trades, arts, business, governmental and educational affairs. Wisdom creates with God, so the more you are filled with wisdom, the more pioneering and creative you become. You will rarely do things the way other people do. *Wisdom is creative power.*

In the Old Covenant, God often enabled skilled men to have wisdom for the construction of those things dedicated to Him in the tabernacle and temple.[207] You need not be smelting golden lampstands and sewing linen tent curtains to tap into this same wisdom. When committed to the Lord, the oil of favor drips from your fingers, causing your hands to prosper in all they do.

---

205 Prov. 3:16, NIV

206 Prov. 4:20-22, NIV

207 See Exod. 28:3

Did you know that wisdom literally puts a tangible glow on your face?

> *Who is like the wise man? Who knows the explanation of things? Wisdom brightens a man's face and changes its hard appearance.*[208]

When you have wisdom, you will *walk safely in your way, and your foot will not stumble.*[209] Are you an insomniac? Obtain wisdom and *your sleep will be sweet.*[210] Wisdom is truly God's *magic potion*! Wisdom is so valuable that the snake oil salesman, Simon the Sorcerer, longed to purchase it from the apostles in Acts 8. He wanted only its external benefits. He was rebuked, because only the Son of God purchases this anointing. It costs more than your money … it cost the Son of God everything He had.

Solomon understood that money would not protect or sustain him. Rather wisdom is *a shelter as money is a shelter.*[211] Did you know that the annual tribute in gold given into Solomon's treasuries each year was 666 talents of gold? It doesn't take a Bible scholar to know that 666 is a wicked number. When we serve money, we are serving mammon. Nevertheless, God knows we have need of material things. The lesson here is this: since Solomon chose not to serve money, money came to serve him! God wants you to be a magnet for material blessing. He wants to make you a resource provider for the nations – funding Kingdom endeavors, giving to

---

[208] Eccles. 8:1, NIV
[209] See Prov. 3:23
[210] See Prov. 3:24
[211] See Eccles. 7:12

the poor and flourishing in generosity. But that only happens when you love Him incomparably more than those riches. There is a true love that never sells out for bottom dollar.

> *If one were to give all the wealth of his house for love, it would be utterly scorned.*[212]

Wisdom always leads you to bear fruits of the Spirit, such as love, kindness, gentleness, etc. The scriptures specifically state that *a man's wisdom gives him patience.*[213] Wisdom also protects you.

One primarily *defensive* facet of wisdom is its ability to preserve you from potential calamity, including the wiles of the ungodly. Scripture tells us, "Wisdom will save you from the ways of wicked men, from men whose words are perverse."[214] It also preserves you from the *seductions of the adulteress* – both literally and figuratively it keeps you chaste from all manner of sin.[215] Wisdom is a defense, and literally becomes a supernatural force field around the life of the Christian. It enables you to "go on your way in safety, and your foot will not stumble; when you lie down, you will not be afraid; when you lie down, your sleep will be sweet. Have no fear of sudden disaster or of the ruin that overtakes the wicked, for the Lord will be your confidence and will keep your foot from being snared."[216]

---

[212] Song of Sol. 8:7, NIV
[213] See Prov. 19:11
[214] Prov. 2:12, NIV
[215] See Prov. 2:16-18
[216] Prov. 3:23-26, NIV

CHAPTER FOUR

+ Wisdom Plays

Due to the severe warnings against those who neglect her, the reader of wisdom literature can sometimes miss the subtle yet solid fact that *wisdom is playful*. Foolishness leads to calamity, but *wisdom is pleasure and relaxation to a man of understanding.*[217] Contrary to modern opinion, wisdom is not confined to stuffy, gray-bearded old men in pullover sweaters smoking ivory pipes. Wisdom *plays*.

There is an essence of the *childlike* that necessarily marks true maturity. And childlikeness is by necessity connected to play and even humor. The Pharisee will, by nature, always be blind to this fact, because of the pompous strutting before men, his rigidity and pretension. The general lack of humility among the professionally religious is itself an object of ridicule and laughable derision by Jesus.

"If it were not the for the medicine of created laughter, there would be no adequate antidote to pride and vanity among men," writes Elton Trueblood author of *The Humor of Christ.*[218]

Those who have read the text of the gospels for years, who are overly comfortable with "the spell of familiar and venerated words," often miss the overt humor of Christ – but a child would notice upon first hearing. When Jesus says that a Pharisee swallows a camel, we may remember an old sermon or familiar exegesis

---

[217] Prov. 10:23, AMP

[218] Elton Trueblood, *The Humor of Christ* (San Francisco: Harper & Row Publishers, 1964), 36.

about that passage. But a child simply laughs when he first hears it. He pictures a massive, hairy animal going down the deacon's throat.

The laughter and playfulness of Christ is not cruel or abusive. Mirth is not the enemy of compassion, nor are laughter and sympathetic concern antithetical. Christ's humor is always redemptive, never mocking the individual. But He is sharp and sarcastic in His derision of those institutions such as Pharisaism, which posture in their self-made self-importance.

Wisdom is not so sober that it loses its joy and childlike wonder. One of the greatest mysteries of the ages is that our God's nature is revelry and play. Our Lord makes it clear in all of the synoptic gospels that unless we become like little children, we will by no means enter the Kingdom of Heaven.[219]

"Any alleged Christianity which fails to express itself in gaiety, at some point, is clearly spurious. The Christian is gay, not because he is blind to injustice and suffering, but because he is convinced that these, in the light of the divine sovereignty, are never *ultimate*," writes Trueblood. "Though he can be sad, and often is perplexed, he is never really worried. The well-known humor of the Christian is not a way of denying the tears, but rather a way of affirming something which is deeper than tears."[220]

---

[219] See Matt. 18:3; Mark 10:15; Luke 18:17

[220] Trueblood, *The Humor of Christ*, 32.

Let us take a moment to look at the playful nature of the Spirit of Wisdom as it is specifically spelled out in scripture.

> *... When He marked out the foundations of the Earth, I (Wisdom) was with Him as someone He could trust. For me, every day was pure delight, as I* ***played in His presence*** *all the time,* ***playing everywhere on His Earth****, and* ***delighting to be with humankind****. Therefore, children, listen to me:* ***happy are those who keep my ways.***[221]

Most scholars have a difficulty in remaining neutral when translating the passage above – probably because it challenges their theology of a *stoic* wisdom. Holy Spirit was literally playing with the Father and throughout the Earth at the dawn of creation. He was even playing with you, His children, before you were ever born! The *Ancient Roots Translinear Old Testament* says it this way:

> *I was day by day His entertainment, reveling in front of Him in all periods, reveling in the land of His world, and my entertainment was the sons of Adam.*[222]

We truly have a good Father who wants to play with us. He takes such pleasure in us, and He is so interested in the affairs of our lives. In His wisdom, He is always growing us and changing us. But nevertheless, He loves us just the way we are.

---

[221] Prov. 8:29-32, CJB

[222] Prov. 8:30-31, ARTB

+ Wisdom or Foolishness?

While the scriptures are adamant to exhort against foolishness, we must remember that this not merely a cultural definition of "foolishness." To the believer, we understand that the fool runs after sin, unrighteous gain, worldly seduction and self-reliance. In our modern, Greco-rationalistic society, we think of foolishness only in terms of slapstick humor or comedic behavior. Anything that is not "rational" is deemed foolish to us. This is not a scriptural definition.

God's definition of foolishness is a polar opposite to the world's definition of folly. He says to rely on the unknown. He says that love conquers all. He says you can't save yourself, so stop trying.

> *For Christ did not send me to baptize, but to preach the gospel—not with words of human wisdom, lest the cross of Christ be emptied of its power. For the message of the cross is foolishness to those who are perishing, but to us who are being saved it is the power of God. For it is written: "I will destroy the wisdom of the wise; the intelligence of the intelligent I will frustrate."*
>
> *Where is the wise man? Where is the scholar? Where is the philosopher of this age? Has not God made foolish the wisdom of the world? For since in the wisdom of God the world through its wisdom did not know Him, God was pleased through the foolishness of what was preached to save those who believe.*[223]

---

[223] 1 Cor. 1:17-21, NIV

To God, wisdom is love hanging on a tree. It boggles the mind. It does not seem to radiate with preeminent signs and wonders. It does not seem to fit into a rational explanation. The Jewish, eastern mind is impressed with miracles. The analytical Greeks of the day were impressed with four-point messages. But God delivered neither of these things to save them – not miracles nor human wisdom. The Pentecostal wants a better miracle service. The Baptist wants an intelligible sermon. Neither will save them. This is what made the apostle Paul such a controversial character. He preached a seemingly ridiculous message that the way to Heaven was through a convict who died on a wooden pole:

> *Jews demand miraculous signs and Greeks look for wisdom, but we preach Christ crucified: a stumbling block to Jews and foolishness to Gentiles, but to those whom God has called, both Jews and Greeks, Christ the power of God and the wisdom of God. For the foolishness of God is wiser than man's wisdom, and the weakness of God is stronger than man's strength.*[224]

In this amazing chapter of scripture, Paul goes on to warn us about taking ourselves too seriously in regard to human wisdom. As a matter of fact, he reminds us to consider when we first were called by God, that "not many of you were wise by human standards."[225] Thanks for the compliment, Paul! He says that most of us were no Einsteins to begin with, nor were many of us very influential. Yet God chose little, insignificant you and I

---

[224] 1 Cor. 1:22-25, NIV

[225] See 1 Cor. 1:26

to showcase the greatest message the world has ever known:

> *But God chose the foolish things of the world to shame the wise; God chose the weak things of the world to shame the strong. He chose the lowly things of this world and the despised things—and the things that are not—to nullify the things that are, so that no one may boast before Him. It is because of Him that you are in Christ Jesus, who has become for us wisdom from God—that is, our righteousness, holiness and redemption. Therefore, as it is written: "Let him who boasts boast in the Lord."*[226]

Not only does the wisdom of this age seek to empty the cross of its power, but also it "loses the climax of salvation history, the revelation of the mystery of God."[227]

+ The Mixed Wine of Wisdom

The Lord continues to flip the tables on our conceptual human wisdom. When one thinks of a wise man, he rarely thinks of a drunkard or an addict. Nevertheless, the very nature of wisdom is to imbibe on the love of God in a supernaturally transcendent way. Wisdom is not overly concerned with the opinions of man, outward appearances, or the objective necessities of running a materially successful ministry, career or suburban lifestyle. Wisdom ravenously hungers for the invisible, eternal God. She thirsts for *new wine*. She may even get

---

226 1 Cor. 1:27-31, NIV

227 Gerald Hawthorne, Ralph Martin, and Daniel Reid, ed., *Dictionary of Paul and His Letters* (Downers Grove, IL: InterVarsity Press, 1993), 970.

rowdy and make an occasional scene at the head of the streets.

Proverbs chapter nine tells us another little known fact about true wisdom. Wisdom *mixes her wine*:

> *Wisdom has built her house, She has hewn out her seven pillars; She has slaughtered her meat,* ***She has mixed her wine****, She has also furnished her table. She has sent out her maidens, She cries out from the highest places of the city, "Whoever is simple, let him turn in here!" As for him who lacks understanding, she says to him, "Come, eat of my bread and* ***drink of the wine I have mixed****.*"[228]

Holy Spirit is, of course, typified as *new wine* in the gospels. The entire New Covenant is symbolized by a cup of something that intoxicates us: real, unfermented wine. But what does it mean in this passage, to say that the Spirit of Wisdom *mixes her wine*? According to Bible commentator Adam Clarke, "probably the *yayin masach*, mingled wine, was wine mingled, not with *water*, to make it *weaker*; but with *spices* and other ingredients to make it *stronger*. The ingredients were *honey, myrrh, mandragora* (an aphrodisiac), *opium*, and such like, which gave it not only an *intoxicating* but *stupifying* quality also. Perhaps the *mixed wine* here may mean *wine* of the *strongest* and *best quality*, that which was good to cheer and refresh the heart of man."[229]

---

228 Prov. 9:1-5, NKJV

229 Clarke, *Commentary on the Whole Bible*, Excerpt from Proverbs 9.

Clarke is basically telling the reader that Holy Spirit has mixed "opiated wine" for us. Of course, God is not endorsing the use of drugs here. Proverbs 20 also tells us that one who mixes wine is *not wise*. Wisdom is not found in the intoxication of natural wine. But rather, Wisdom is the Wine of God's Spirit. This is symbolic of the highest degrees of a transcendent, divine intimacy available to us in Christ. Myrrh is literally a psychoactive drug. As *Peloubet's Bible Dictionary* confirms, myrrh is "a highly fragrant resin and volatile oil used as a cosmetic, and stimulative as a medicine."[230] Remember that Jesus refused to drink the wine mixed with myrrh while hanging on the cross. He does not promote drug use. It is Christ Himself who is the wine, dripping with myrrh. Myrrh is the oil used for embalming. It represents the actual death of Christ. What really intoxicates us is not merely the revelation that the *life is in the blood*. But also, that *our own death to self* was in His body! On the cross, He eliminated the old, boring, soberly religious you! He cut away your old sinful self, and you are free to enjoy a whole new existence in Him.

Other scholars confirm that the mixed wine was "made stronger and more inebriating by the addition of higher and more powerful ingredients, such as honey, spices, myrrh, mandragora, opiates, and other strong drugs."[231] What is of further interest is that Lord tells His bride that her *navel is like a round goblet that never lacks spiced wine.*[232] Your belly – your inmost being – is

[230] F.N. Peloubet, *Peloubet's Bible Dictionary* (New York: Holt, Rinehart and Winston, Inc., 1947), 429.

[231] James M. Freeman, *The New Manners and Customs of the Bible* (Alachua, FL: Bridge Logos, 1998).

[232] Song of Sol. 7:2, CJB

fully and continually filled with this blissful drink of divine love.

Have you ever felt so spiritually rapt, almost physically absorbed and pulled outside of yourself when a teacher of great wisdom opened the scriptures to you? Then you have drank of the mixed wine. Just as the apostles appeared drunk and beside themselves in Acts 2 when the Spirit came, so does wisdom breed ecstatic experience that often appears outwardly foolish to the uninitiated.

Wisdom serves new wine, and she serves ancient mysteries. Prophetic teacher Rick Joyner says, "The Lord is 'the wise man who brings forth from His treasures things both new and old.' The Lord does have new wine to serve, but Isaiah 25:6 declares that the Lord will also serve 'refined, aged wine.' The Lord will not use either the old or the new, but both the old and new."[233]

+ Natural Wisdom

The wisdom of this world contrasts the wisdom of Heaven as much as the Tree of Knowledge contrasts the Tree of Life. When Eve *saw that the fruit of the tree was good for food and pleasing to the eye, and also desirable for gaining wisdom, she took some and ate it.*[234] It is not wrong to desire wisdom. When satan first foiled humanity, he appealed to a valid desire in the heart of mankind: *to be like God.* The truth is that man

---

233 "War and Glory," *MorningStar Journal*, Vol. 4, No. 2 (Charlotte: Morningstar Publications, Inc.), 56-65.

234 See Gen. 3:6

was already made in God's image. Furthermore, it is valid that we become God-like. We are all to be conformed to the image of Christ. The problem comes when we try to do it *ourselves*.

It is not arrogance to want to imitate the Beautiful One. That is only natural. Arrogance comes into play when we attempt this with our own religious efforts. This is why satan fell. He said:

> *I will ascend to heaven; I will raise my throne above the stars of God; I will sit enthroned on the mount of assembly, on the utmost heights of the sacred mountain. I will ascend above the tops of the clouds; I will make myself like the Most High.*[235]

There's nothing wrong with being in Heaven or sitting on the sacred mountain. That's where you already are, thanks to the work of the cross.[236] The problem for satan is the same problem for religionists. It's the insistence of saying, "I will."

Religion idolizes the volition of the human will. It wants you to make yourself holy. Ascend the mountain. You see this in every denominational stream. We see that satan was jealous, competitive with the other angels (stars) and obviously proud. But the consistent theme of his diatribe is to *do it himself*. It is an utter self-reliance and independence from God that brings about his catastrophic fall. Whatever human system of regulation or attempt at outer holiness that religion contrives, it will never add anything to the perfect work of

---

[235] Isa. 14:13-14, NIV

[236] See Eph. 2:6

the cross. There is an appearance of wisdom, or godliness, that is based solely on human regulation, but "there is no wisdom, no insight, no plan that can succeed against the Lord."[237]

> *I know that these regulations look wise with their self-inspired efforts at worship, their policy of self-humbling, and their studied neglect of the body. But in actual practice they do honor, not to God, but to man's own pride.*[238]

+ Wisdom Brings Authority

The life of King Solomon provides us priceless insight into the nature of wisdom – particularly the authority proffered those who obtain it. We are all familiar with the story of his encounter with the Lord, when he first requested this impartation:

> *God said to Solomon, "Since this is your heart's desire and you have not asked for wealth, riches or honor, nor for the death of your enemies, and since you have not asked for a long life but for wisdom and knowledge to govern my people over whom I have made you king, therefore wisdom and knowledge will be given you. And I will also give you wealth, riches and honor, such as no king who was before you ever had and none after you will have."*[239]

---

[237] Prov. 21:30, NIV
[238] Col. 2:23, PHI
[239] 2 Chron. 1:11-12, NIV

Solomon chose wisdom over money, natural authority and prestige. The result is that he received it all. He was endued with wisdom. But as a byproduct, he acquired mass wealth. He not only built his own house, but the House of the Lord. He was honored with great prestige among the nations, and even his enemies made peace with him.

> *The Lord gave Solomon wisdom, just as He had promised him. There were peaceful relations between Hiram and Solomon, and the two of them made a treaty.*[240]

Wisdom never promises that you will be *without* enemies, but it does enable you to live at peace with them. Those who heed wisdom's voice will *live in safety and be at ease, without fear of harm.*[241] This is part of wisdom's favor, for *when a man's ways please the Lord, He makes even his enemies to be at peace with him.*[242]

Wisdom brings with it an authority to build, which is rooted in favor with God and man. We learn from Solomon that, when you possess it, people come from afar to seek your wisdom.[243] People are drawn to you. You are respected. People volunteer freely, just to glean from the fruit of your lips. It is easy to walk in authority when you have good employees! The scriptures tell us that Solomon's servants were *happy to stand before him.*[244]

---

240 1 Kings 5:12, NIV

241 See Prov. 1:33

242 See Prov. 16:7

243 See 1 Kings 10:24

244 See 1 Kings 10:8

Since Solomon owned the hill of finance, it gave him massive sway in civil affairs. He covered everything in gold. Silver was as worthless as pebbles on the ground during his reign. He was the richest man on the planet. When the Queen of Sheba came to visit Solomon, his depth of insight floored her. The riches were so extravagant; she finally became sick just looking at the cutlery and the ornate detail of the waiters' clothes. She said that not half of it had been told to her.

Solomon did not earn these things. It wasn't even his fault that he made the right request from the Lord! The night he asked for wisdom, he probably just got lucky. The Lord in His grace caused Solomon to ask for the right thing from Him.

The irony of wisdom is that it never seeks its own authority. In the Kingdom, the greatest must be the servant of all. Like Solomon's father David, we must never seek to acquire power by our own means – even when it is within our grasp to take it. David could have killed Saul for a shortcut into the palace, but he didn't. Just because the fruit was within Eve's grasp doesn't mean it was wise to eat. It takes wisdom to obtain wisdom. Wisdom understands that unless the Lord builds the house, the workers labor in vain.

+ Apostolic Master Builders

Wisdom has built her house; she has hewn out its seven pillars. She has prepared meat and mixed her wine; she has also set her table.[245]

---

[245] Prov. 9:1-2, NIV

Truly, God Himself must build our spiritual house. Moreover, He must *become* the house – He is both the foundation and the finishing capstone. He is its seven pillars of support. Furthermore, without the depths of wisdom, we will never encounter the meatier things of the word, or the intoxicating wine of His presence. It is wisdom to embrace both the strong meat (the Word) and the strong wine (the Spirit). True ministry building is never about bigger programs, cathedrals or news lists. It is about growing in the anointing and building hearts.

Wisdom is always a prerequisite in the anointing for leadership. This applies not only to ministers, but also to those who are called to civil authority in the secular arena. Consider the qualifications for selecting the first seven deacons of the church.

> *Brothers, choose seven men from among you who are known to be full of the Spirit and wisdom. We will turn this responsibility over to them.*[246]

In those days, the church was practicing a type of *holy communism*. The deacons held both a spiritual authority and a natural management of feeding everybody. This required them to be Spirit-filled, and to possess wisdom. In the church, we are all kings and priests, holding both natural and spiritual authority. Let us be full of the Spirit and wisdom!

The Lord is releasing a generation of apostolic *master builders* in these days. But the question is whether we are going to pursue our own goals, platforms and kingdoms – or will we advance *His* Kingdom. Furthermore,

---

[246] Acts 6:3, NIV

if it is His Kingdom we want furthered, are we going to let Him do it through us, or foolishly try to help Him out?

With much authority comes much responsibility. The moment we attempt to shoulder that responsibility ourselves, we have traded the place of intimacy for dead works. *The government rests on His shoulders.* The only real vocation for a Christian is to abide in the womb of the morning.

+ SOLOMON'S FOLLIES

Consider the prestige that was afforded to Solomon. The Bible says that *every king* of the Earth sought audience with him, *to hear the wisdom God had put in his heart.* In fact, everyone in the whole world sought audience with Solomon – not for a handout, but just to listen to His wisdom![247]

Now imagine how much authority this one individual carried over the entire Earth, centuries before Pentecost. At best, he was operating in just one or two of the sevenfold flows of Holy Spirit – chiefly the wisdom that was put in his heart. But you – as a New Covenant believer – have the fullness of God living inside of you. Whatever would it look like for a man to really believe that and manifest that?

Solomon was a man who was given everything by earthly standards. He had favor with God and man. Wisdom brings both praise and honor from men.[248] Of

---

[247] 2 Chron. 9:23; 1 Kings 10:24 NIV

[248] See Prov. 3:35; 12:8

course, this is a mixed blessing. You will never be hurt by the criticism of men if you never seek the praises of men.

Surely Solomon's wisdom provoked a massive thirst for *more* in his heart. At the end of his life he conceded to his vain quest for *more*, admitting that he had run up many blind alleys, having never found what he was looking for.

In his day, however, he was the wisest man on the face of the Earth. Consequently, he also wrote the most intimate book of the Bible, the Song of Songs. I believe that wisdom awakened great love within him that could never be satiated apart from God. At that point, Solomon had gone too far to take his eyes off the Lord. There comes a time in your Christian walk, when your heart has just been opened too far by God. The more you walk with Him, the more He expands your soul to receive more of Him. Your capacity for intimacy and pleasure get so enlarged – your appetites are too big for anything the world has to offer. If a person turned from God at that point in the game, the headlong plunge into sin could be heinous and most severe. The palate that is accustomed to feasting on God would turn to ravenous extremes if trying feed in the trough of the world.

Solomon's folly thrust him straight into idolatry. He amassed hundreds of wives and concubines, who drew him to foreign gods until the repentance of his latter years. Wisdom provokes a deeper thirst in us. God alone can satisfy it.

+ The Coming Wise Men

Regardless of his seasonal failings, the Glory that was afforded under Solomon's reign was amazing. God revealed Himself quite openly and tangibly. When Solomon dedicated the temple, the heavy "kabod" weight of God's Glory – His tangible presence – rested so strongly on the priests that they were unable to stand to minister.

Wisdom ushers in the Glory of God, and "the wise shall inherit Glory."[249]

Beyond precepts and the letter of the law, wisdom's chief aim is to usher us into the very tangible substance of God's manifest presence. We can all abide in that place of intimate union which such palpable intensity that the very substance of God drips from our fingertips and radiates from our pores. We were created for this realm of Glory.

Over the years, prophetic teacher Rick Joyner has often pointed to the following prophecy of our Lord:

> *Therefore, indeed, I send you prophets, wise men, and scribes: some of them you will kill and crucify, and some of them you will scourge in your synagogues and persecute from city to city.*[250]

He makes a profound delineation between *prophets, wise men* and *scribes*. Prophets bring revelation. Scribes are anointed writers. But Joyner says we have

---

[249] Prov. 3:35, NKJV

[250] Matt. 23:34, NKJV

not yet seen the full release of the *wise men*, which bring wisdom in the building of apostolic ministry.

What will these wise men look like? I tell you they will not be college professors in tweed jackets. If they are anything similar to Solomon in all his splendor, Daniel in Babylon or Joseph in Egypt – we will see a mantle of authority on them that shakes nations, bends the knees of rulers and ushers the Glory of God into entire regions.

The strength of these men will be as powerful as all their oppressors and persecutors multiplied together. The Book of Ecclesiastes says, "*Wisdom makes one wise man more powerful than ten rulers in a city.*"[251]

Often we think of our patriarchs – Abraham, Isaac and Jacob – as dirty shepherds wandering about Palestine. But don't you know that they were filthy rich? Abraham and Lot were so prosperous; they had to take two separate countries! Abraham defeated five kings and owned the wealth of more than five nations. They were overrunning with servants, flocks – people and families – and enormous amounts of gold.

The church has shied away from macroeconomics, surrendering the mountain of world economics to the idolatrous and the ungodly. Most Christians get paranoid at the thought of big money. They consider the world financial sector only to be the prerogative of the antichrist and the mark of the beast.

---

[251] Eccles. 7:19, NIV

What will it look like when we see wise men emerging again, who carry both natural and spiritual authority? Abraham, Isaac and Jacob encountered God. With one prayer, Abraham once healed an entire nation. They moved in the supernatural. God made them *famous for their bliss*, and wanted the nations to be envious of their blessings. The Earth is about to see certain ones emerging who will righteously manage billions of dollars ... and they will also work miracles.

+ Obtain Wisdom

Wisdom cannot be earned or learned, but it must be received and cherished. We must learn to embrace wisdom and ask for it, for "*if any of you lacks wisdom, he should ask God, who gives generously to all without finding fault, and it will be given to him.*"[252] God only allows man to diligently hunger for a thing if it is somehow an extension of Himself. For God alone is worthy of adoration. This is why we are permitted to "*follow the way of love and* ***eagerly desire*** *spiritual gifts, especially the gift of prophecy.*"[253] The gifts can be desired because they are simply expressions of Jesus. The testimony of Jesus *is* the Spirit of Prophecy, so we can desire to prophesy. We can seek gifts of healing because Jesus *is* the Healer. He is healing itself. These are extensions of His nature.

The same is true of wisdom. He is "*Christ Jesus, who has become for us wisdom from God.*"[254] Therefore, our

---

[252] Jas. 1:5, NIV

[253] 1 Cor. 14:1, NIV

[254] 1 Cor. 1:30, NIV

pursuit of wisdom is tantamount to our pursuit of God Himself.

So how do we get wisdom? *Simply ask.* But you must ask believing.

> *But let him ask in faith, nothing wavering. For he that wavereth is like a wave of the sea driven with the wind and tossed. For let not that man think that he shall receive any thing of the Lord. A double minded man is unstable in all his ways.*[255]

The *asking* element is not supposed to be a human *work*. It is just an admission of dependence. How quickly we turn everything into self-effort! James is putting the emphasis on God's ability to provide. Faith is the key element here. Trust that God will enlighten you with wisdom, even as you already possess the person of Wisdom within you! Paul constantly asked for wisdom, not merely for himself but for others:

> *For this reason, since the day we heard about you, we have not stopped praying for you and* ***asking God*** *to fill you with the knowledge of His will through all spiritual wisdom and understanding.*[256]

+ The Impartation of Wisdom

The fact that wisdom is a gift from above is further highlighted by the fact that it can literally be *imparted* from one person to another. It is not just memorized

---

[255] Jas. 1:6-8, KJV

[256] Col. 1:9, NIV

from seminary books. Wisdom, like faith, has *substance.*

> *Now Joshua son of Nun was filled with the spirit of wisdom because Moses had laid his hands on him.*[257]

The laying on of hands activates things. It opens doors. But if you want wisdom, it doesn't hurt to read your Bible a bit as well!

There are a number of things that activate wisdom in your life. Proverbs – or spiritual teachings – are given *for attaining wisdom and discipline; for understanding words of insight.*[258] In the same way, one gains wisdom by heeding a father's instruction.[259] Other wise men impart wisdom through their sayings.[260]

A basic tool for giving wisdom is *discipline.* In today's church, it is hard to use the word "discipline," without conjuring up images of lots of hard work. I do not refer to striving spiritual exercises. Nor do I refer to *punishment.* I simply refer to a father's discipline as he thumps a child's hand to prevent him from burning it on the stove.

> *The rod of correction imparts wisdom, but a child left to himself disgraces his mother.*[261]

---

257 Deut. 34:9, NIV

258 See Prov. 1:2

259 See Prov. 2:1; 3:1; 4:1; 5:1

260 See Prov. 10:13; 10:31

261 Prov. 29:15, NIV

God's discipline is always gracious, patient and kind toward us. In fact, His entire law was just a school master used to point us to His grace. God only disciplines us to keep us in a place of pure pleasure. It is imperative to continually listen to wisdom's correction, as it brings an outpouring of God's heart and thoughts.

> *If you had responded to my rebuke, I would have poured out my heart to you and made my thoughts known to you.*[262]

Consequently, wisdom literature is replete with dire warnings if we reject her correction. Ignoring her puts us in a position of never finding wisdom when we need her most.

The hardened heart cannot hear her voice.

> *... when calamity overtakes you like a storm, when disaster sweeps over you like a whirlwind, when distress and trouble overwhelm you. ... they will call to me but I will not answer; they will look for me but will not find me.*[263]

We first receive wisdom by means of the fear of the Lord – this is the beginning of wisdom. But the fear of the Lord also continues to *teach a man wisdom.*[264]

We also obtain wisdom through *humility.*

---

[262] Prov. 1:23, NIV

[263] Prov. 1:27-28, NIV

[264] See Prov. 9:10; 15:33; Ps. 111:10

CHAPTER FOUR

When pride comes, then comes disgrace, but with humility comes wisdom.[265]

The basic premise of Christianity that sets us apart from every other belief system on the planet is the admission of our absolute inability to better ourselves. Our initiation rite is a confession of complete failure and acknowledgement of utter dependence on God.

The beauty of humility is found not in the obsession over personal transgressions. Its wonder lies in the simple fact that our gaze has turned off from ourselves altogether. The eyes are no longer locked on self – they are now free to stare into His eternal splendor. You are no longer "wise in your own eyes," but instead, have learned to "trust in the Lord with all your heart and lean not on your own understanding."[266]

The flavor of humility is joy, because we can laugh at ourselves and not take our own role or ministry too seriously.

He who trusts in himself is a fool, but he who walks in wisdom is kept safe.[267]

Ultimately, all wisdom stems from God's grace and no effort of our own, *for the Lord gives wisdom, and from His mouth come knowledge and understanding.*[268] It is birthed from a place of simple reliance and intimacy with God, where He teaches us wisdom in the inmost

---

[265] Prov. 11:2, NIV
[266] See Prov. 3:7; 3:5
[267] Prov. 28:26, NIV
[268] See Prov. 2:6

parts. He gives it to those who please Him. But to sinners He gives the task of gathering and storing up wealth for the man who pleases God.[269]

+ Wisdom and the Sevenfold

It is clear from many verses we have already read that wisdom is specifically intertwined with the other seven Spirits. For starters, we have read that it begins with the fear of the Lord. Interestingly we find all seven of the Spirits listed in connection to wisdom within the following passage of Proverbs:

> ***I, wisdom**, dwell with prudence, and find out **knowledge** and discretion. **The fear of the Lord** is to hate evil; pride and arrogance and the evil way and the perverse mouth I hate. **Counsel** is mine, and sound wisdom; I am **understanding**, I have **strength**.*[270]

We have noted the sevenfold connection in Proverbs 9:1 as well, as *wisdom has built her house; she has hewn out her **seven pillars**.*

Besides the center lamp – the Spirit of the Lord – wisdom is personified in scripture more than any of the other six branches of lampstand.

+ The Spirit of Understanding

Let's now move to the Spirit of Understanding, which is so closely paired together with wisdom.

---

[269] See Eccles. 2:26

[270] Prov. 8:12-14, NKJV

Wisdom, "chokmah," is skill, dexterity, comprehension of various learning, piety towards God and is often ascribed toward a ruler or king.[271]

Understanding, "biynah," is comprehension as in understanding a language or as to become intelligent. It is an ability to put the pieces of a puzzle together.[272]

Wisdom is "in its highest form implying comprehension of the secret things of God," according to one commentator. Understanding, on the other hand, is "keen, quick discernment; the sagacity which discovers the right thing to do, and the right word to say."[273]

Wisdom often has to do with receiving, listening or attentiveness to the Word by the *ear*. And understanding has to do with comprehending or meditating on a word in the *heart*.

> *My son, if you* ***receive my words****, and* ***treasure my commands*** *within you, so that you incline your* ***ear to wisdom****, and apply your* ***heart to understanding****.*[274] ...

Of course, these word pictures of "ear" and "heart" are not consistent. For instance, in some verses, it is understanding which pertains to the ears: *Lend your ear to My understanding.*[275]

---

271 Strong, *Exhaustive Concordance of the Bible*, Entry 2451.
272 Ibid., Entry 998.
273 Spence and Exell, ed., *The Pulpit Commentary: Isaiah*, Vol. 1.
274 Prov. 2:1-2, NKJV
275 Prov. 5:1, NKJV

In a sense, understanding is the unpackaging of the wisdom that is received. There are countless verses that pair wisdom and understanding together. Not the least of which is this one, which delineate their different roles:

> *By wisdom a house is built, and through understanding it is established; through knowledge its rooms are filled with rare and beautiful treasures.*[276]

Wisdom comes by faith, and likewise, *by faith we understand.*[277] Just like wisdom, understanding is imparted through teaching and proverbs.[278] Like wisdom, understanding also releases favor.[279] Together, they are better than silver, gold or rubies, and the Book of Proverbs says, "all the things you may desire cannot compare with her."[280]

So many of the attributes of wisdom are likewise found in understanding – as well as its many benefits. Length of days, riches and honor, paths of peace as well as pleasantness and happiness are all shared traits between the two.[281]

Like wisdom, understanding is both personalized, and implicitly feminine in scripture:

---

[276] Prov. 24:3-4, NIV

[277] See Heb. 11:3

[278] See Prov. 1:2

[279] See Prov. 13:15

[280] Prov. 3:15, NKJV

[281] See Prov. 3:16-18

> *Say to wisdom, "You are my sister," and* ***call understanding your nearest kin.***[282]

> *Does not wisdom cry out, and* ***understanding lift up her voice?***[283]

Interestingly, the Spirit of Wisdom releases or *activates* understanding in the believer's life through communion with Jesus. Notice the symbology of the bread and the wine here:

> *As for him who lacks understanding, she says to him, "Come, eat of my bread and drink of the wine I have mixed. ..."*[284]

While we do not have time to highlight each and every pairing of wisdom and understanding, here are just a few examples of how they interact. As you will see, the two are virtually inseparable:

> *Wisdom is found on the lips of him who has understanding. ...*[285]

> *Wisdom rests in the heart of him who has understanding. ...*[286]

> *Wisdom is in the sight of him who has understanding. ...*[287]

---

[282] Prov. 7:4, NKJV
[283] Prov. 8:1, NKJV
[284] Prov. 9:4-5, NKJV
[285] Prov. 10:13, NKJV
[286] Prov. 14: 33, NKJV
[287] Prov. 17:24, NKJV

WISDOM AND UNDERSTANDING

In speaking of wisdom and understanding, John Wesley says, "It is not needful, exactly to distinguish these two gifts; it is sufficient that they are necessary qualifications for a governor, and a teacher, and it is evident they signify perfect knowledge of all things necessary for his own and peoples good, and a sound judgment, to distinguish between things that differ."[288]

While it is not necessary to implicitly distinguish between wisdom and understanding, we should note that God can empower your understanding supernaturally. Daniel – a man renowned for these two virtues – was given "skill to understand."[289] It is possible for you to receive this very same impartation! Consider Daniel's ability to receive visions, interpret dreams and access revelatory abilities. This is all implicitly connected with understanding.

Understanding deals largely with interpretation of the unseen realm. Think of it in terms of the ability to *understand* a language such as French, Polish or Portuguese. Understanding is highly interpretative. It is also connected to one's comprehension.

Understanding, like wisdom is an impartation breathed into you by God. Like your very pulse, understanding is one of the vital signs that show you are alive.

> *But it is the spirit in a man, the breath of the Almighty, that gives him understanding.*[290]

---

288 Wesley, *John Wesley's Notes on the Whole Bible: The New Testament*, Notes on Isaiah.

289 See Dan. 9:22

290 Job 32:8, NIV

CHAPTER FOUR

+ A Third Cord of Discernment

To another way to define "understanding" is to consider the word in this context: *Jesus understands what I am going through*. He is a sympathetic High Priest in Heaven.[291] It is the understanding of God that enables Him to empathize with humanity. He has walked in our shoes. Christ has a perfect understanding of men's hearts. He is not duped by outward appearances, because *He shall not judge by the sight of His eyes, nor decide by the hearing of His ears*.[292] Jesus discerned the extravagance of the widow's offering, though it only appeared to be two mites. He was also quick to sniff out a hypocrite, and was not impressed with their outward forms of holiness. His discernment is perfect.

Understanding is paralleled quite often in scripture with the virtue of *discernment*. Discernment literally means to "taste." We can rightly discern good from evil by *tasting the difference* between the two. It is a spiritual sensory perception.

> *But solid food is for the mature, who by constant use have trained themselves to discern good from evil.*[293]

Along with tasting, discernment also implies to "separate," as in possessing the ability to rightly separate or *divide the word of God*. It implies a separation between light and darkness. Discernment and understanding do mature with age and experience. We learn what tastes

---

[291] See Heb. 4:15-16

[292] See Isa. 11:3

[293] Heb. 5:14, NIV

good, and what tastes bad. If we just eat anything, any word that comes our way, that's a major failure in discernment.

Discernment should never devolve into paranoia, as it has in many Christian circles. In fact, under the guise of using "discernment" Christians accuse, cast out or crucify any new thing they don't understand in many churches. Love always trusts. Suspicion is not a fruit of the Spirit. Just because someone has a "check in their spirit," a "red flag," or a "concern" about something, does not mean they are right. They are just uncomfortable. God loves to make us uncomfortable. I'm sure a red flag would pop up if Isaiah walked naked up to the altar of your church!

True discernment is not about pointing out evil, recognizing devils or exposing the demonic. True discernment is being able to *see the Lord* in a situation. Any immature believer with a blog and this *gift of paranoia* can have their own ministry on the Internet, ignorantly bashing their brothers. Perhaps this is one reason the apostle Paul says though you have ten thousand teachers you do not have many fathers.[294]

+ Understanding Reconciles

The opposite of understanding is *misunderstanding*. Misunderstanding is satan's key for division. This is how he breaks relationships, splits churches and deceives people. The root of our misunderstanding comes from the fall. In the Garden of Eden, sin entered, and satan's main strategy was to break relationship between

---

[294] See 1 Cor. 4:15

man and God. His first target of attack was to challenge the existing *communication* lines, asking "Did God say?"

Yet from the foundation of the world, God had made a plan to restore this relationship. It pleased Him to bruise His own son, that we might come closer to Him than Adam ever walked. Now we, like the apostle Paul, have now been entrusted with a "ministry of reconciliation" to turn hearts back to God. By allowing the fullness of the Spirit of Wisdom and Understanding to flow through our lives, it makes a powerful decree even to atmospheric powers and principalities.

> *His intent was that now, through the church, the manifold wisdom of God should be made known to the rulers and authorities in the heavenly realms.*[295]

Christ continues to speak through us, declaring the good news of reconciliation with God, reopening the doors of communication and reversing *mis*-understanding in the world. He reveals Himself now through the church. As His lampstand, He speaks to us saying *you are the light of the world.*[296]

The Lord was never satisfied with a few prophets. He wants a prophetic people, flowing with an unceasing river of revelation. Everything you say can now be honey dripping copiously from the comb. Peter writes, "if **anyone speaks**, he should do it as one speaking the very words of God."[297]

---

[295] Eph. 3:10, NIV

[296] See Matt. 5:14

[297] See I Pet. 4:11

Christ is the restoration of divine communication.

Now that Jesus has broken down the wall of separation, divine revelation is no longer reserved for the spiritually "elite." Even a child can hear His voice. He says, "My sheep listen to my voice; I know them, and they follow me."[298]

+ Revelatory Realms

We have noted at the onset of the chapter that the Spirit of Wisdom and Understanding is a river of revelation that far outweighs the prophetic gifts of 1 Corinthians 12. People use the word "prophecy" to generally describe all of the following revelatory gifts:

A ***word of knowledge*** is a divine piece of information or fact.

A ***word of wisdom*** is a divine piece of direction into the plan, purpose or will of God.

Prophecy in its basic sense is usually future telling.

Discernment of spirits is an ability to rightly recognize good or evil influences.

Interpretation is the ability to understand or translate dreams, visions or tongues.

These are all wonderful and valid gifts that the Lord wants us to receive, exercise and use. However, the sevenfold is not merely a gift. *It is God Himself.* Imag-

---

298 See John 10:27

ine not just a word of wisdom, but *river of wisdom* that flows through you, possesses you and absolutely overtakes you. Instead of you controlling wisdom, wisdom comes to control you.

Over the past forty years, God has restored much insight to the church regarding the prophetic gifts. Unfortunately, many people still view the gifts as tools on their tool belt, which they can sporadically use at their own whim and pleasure. There is a place far beyond these gifts. There is a higher plane of living where *God possesses you*! He is looking to put you on His tool belt and use you at His whim and pleasure!

You will not need to "pray for a word" or put your gift into operation once this river overtakes you. Everywhere you go and everything you do will be deluged with revelation.

Flowing through your members is a wellspring of revelation that the ancients longed to discover. Jesus said, "For I tell you the truth, many prophets and righteous men longed to see what you see but did not see it, and to hear what you hear but did not hear it."[299] You do not just have a word of wisdom or word of knowledge coming to you. Not just a sporadic prophetic utterance. You have the very Son of God flowing and bursting through you!

> *In the past God spoke to our forefathers through the prophets at many times and in various ways, but in these last days He has spoken to us by His Son.*[300]

---

[299] See Matt. 13:17

[300] Heb. 1:1-2, NIV

New Testament believers are more powerful than the greatest Old Covenant prophets, because we now have the indwelling of Holy Spirit. The blood of the Lamb has opened prophecy up to all. It has opened up the treasuries of His riches and the wellsprings of His power. Beyond all else, we have *hope*. In the Old Testament, prophets called to repent merely to avoid judgment. In the New Covenant, we call people to repentance that they might return to mercy and be restored to God. This is a subtle but important difference.

Under the Old Covenant, prophets highlighted the sin in the people. New Covenant prophets point out the righteousness of Christ in His people, that they might manifest their true identity. Old Testament prophets told of a future breakthrough. New Testament prophets point backward to the reality of what Christ has once and for all accomplished.

The Spirit of Wisdom and Understanding – which is synonymous with the Spirit of Revelation – brings a supernatural opening of our eyes to the unseen things. We no longer discern by natural sight or by human wisdom. After listing the sevenfold anointing of God, Isaiah speaks of Christ in the next verse of chapter 11:

> *He will not judge by what He sees with His eyes, or decide by what He hears with His ears. ...*[301]

The Spirit of Wisdom and Revelation opens our eyes to heavenly realities. Unless our spirits are awakened, our eyes and ears will be closed to discern God's voice. The

[301] Isa. 11:3b, NIV

Bible calls this a veil of stupor – quite literally, it is a *spirit of stupidity.*

Speaking of Israel, who did not recognize Messiah, Paul says, "God gave them a spirit of stupor, eyes so that they could not see and ears so that they could not hear, to this very day."[302]

Through sin and wounding, we had all lost spiritual sensitivity, causing us to reject God's presence. Continual resistance to His Spirit caused us to be hardened further:

> *Make the heart of this people calloused; make their ears dull and close their eyes. Otherwise they might see with their eyes, hear with their ears, understand with their hearts, and turn and be healed.*[303]

The eyes of our heart are only opened through the death of Christ on the cross, as He alone tore the veil of separation between God and humanity. The veil is actually affected through the law – through our own self-efforts toward religious righteousness. It is the veil that still covers the mind of the Jews when Moses is read today.[304] But now, Moses is dead and we have entered into the Promise Land.

In the New Testament, I personally believe that the Apostle Paul was referring to the joint operation of wisdom and understanding when he wrote the following verse:

---

[302] Rom. 11:8, NIV
[303] Isa. 6:10, NIV
[304] See 2 Cor. 3:15

I keep asking that the God of our Lord Jesus Christ, the glorious Father, may give you the ***Spirit of wisdom and revelation****, so that you may know Him better. I pray also that the eyes of your heart may be enlightened in order that you may know the hope to which He has called you, the riches and glorious inheritance in the saints, and His incomparable great power for us who believe.*[305]

It is worth repeating that the Spirits of Wisdom and Revelation come as an impartation. This is not merely something gained from books or study, but in a supernatural transaction, you pick this up. It is a tangible, transferrable anointing that comes from the cross of Christ and can be passed along as "shared faith" from one person to another. The primary avenue of cultivation is through our daily, one-on-one enjoyment of the Lord.

We gaze on God not with our natural eyes, but our spiritual eyes. These "eyes of the heart" are activated in the Secret Place. Intimacy is paramount to seeing. We drink in His love, which causes us to love more. We are able to love, only because He first loved us. A strictly "functional" prophet that receives information without a heart of love is worthless.

If I have the gift of prophecy and can fathom all mysteries and all knowledge, and if I have a faith that can move mountains, but have not love, I am nothing.[306]

---

[305] Eph. 1:11-19, NIV

[306] 1 Cor. 13:2, NIV

Remember that the eyes speak of our gaze. What are we gazing at? What are we meditating on? Whatever consumes our thoughts and our focus is the very place where our heart is.

We become what we gaze upon. Christ's heart is stolen when we gaze upon Him.

> *You have stolen my heart, my sister, my bride; you have stolen my heart with one glance of your eyes, with one jewel of your necklace.*[307]

The greatest mysteries of God have now been unveiled to the simplest believer. There is no longer any shroud or enigma that blocks us from the deep things of God. All of the mysteries of Heaven have been plainly revealed in Christ.

> *No eye has seen, no ear has heard, no mind has conceived what God has prepared for those who love Him" –* ***but God has revealed it to us by His Spirit****. The Spirit searches all things,* ***even the deep things of God.***[308]

The Apostle Paul wished that we "may become progressively more intimately acquainted with and may know more definitely and accurately and thoroughly that mystic secret of God, [which is] Christ (the Anointed One)."[309]

Christ Himself is the *mystic secret*. He is overjoyed and

---

[307] Song of Sol. 4:9, NIV
[308] 1 Cor. 2:9-11, NIV
[309] Col. 2:2, AMP

delighted to be revealed to such simple creatures as ourselves! Yes, Jesus is brimming over with happiness to expose His mysteries to childlike believers.

> *At that time Jesus, full of joy through the Holy Spirit, said, "I praise you, Father, Lord of Heaven and Earth, because you have hidden these things from the wise and learned, and revealed them to little children. Yes, Father, for this was your good pleasure."*[310]

Have you ever read the scriptures and it seemed like reading Chinese? As a young boy, I attended a very legalistic church and was dutifully forced to read my Bible out of obligation. Although I spent years reading it, bits at a time – I could somehow *never comprehend* anything I read! I was not an ignorant child. I made excellent grades and even attended accelerated classes. But somehow, when I tried to read the scriptures, a tangible veil seemed to come over my eyes. I spent years trying to read it, but somehow the words just seemed garbled and unintelligible – as if I were listening to Charlie Brown's teacher.

It was not until years later, in college, when I turned to Christ, that I was instantly transformed and filled with Holy Spirit in a moment. Suddenly, the Spirit of Revelation came and opened my eyes. The thing that amazed me was that I had an immediate, supernatural grasp of the scriptures. I could look at one verse and see hundreds of truths in it, as if a single sentence held thousands upon thousands of hyperlinks to new dimensions of understanding. I could see into the *living Word*, as if

---

[310] Luke 10:21, NIV

the Bible itself was a pulsing, breathing machine. Every fiber and sinew of each verse was connected. I could somehow see that if even one jot or letter were removed from it, the entire universe would fall apart.

As a child, I had never fully turned to the Christ of the scriptures. I had read the words of the Bible, never fully recognizing how they all pointed to Him – this present and living Deity. For all those years, I had been reading the scriptures just as the Jews had read the law and the prophets – blinded by a veil of ignorance and law.

> *But their minds were made dull, for to this day the same veil remains when the old covenant is read. It has not been removed, because only in Christ is it taken away. Even to this day when Moses is read, a veil covers their hearts. But whenever anyone turns to the Lord, the veil is taken away.*[311]

The love of Christ enables us to understand Him.

+ Wisdom & Understanding Hidden

There is a secretive nature about wisdom and understanding that intrigues the mystics of the faith. The Book of Job tells us of men who search in the bowels of the Earth, digging through the farthest recesses in blackest darkness in search for silver and gold, copper and sapphires. Far from the dwellings of people, these men cut shafts into the rocks, searching in the roots of the mountains.

---

[311] 2 Cor. 3:14-16, NIV

> *But where can wisdom be found? Where does understanding dwell? Man does not comprehend its worth; it cannot be found in the land of the living. The deep says, "It is not in me"; the sea says, "It is not with me." It cannot be bought with the finest gold, nor can its price be weighed in silver. ... Where then does wisdom come from? Where does understanding dwell? It is hidden from the eyes of every living thing, concealed even from the birds of the air. Destruction and Death say, "Only a rumor of it has reached our ears." God understands the way to it and He alone knows where it dwells.*[312]

The apprehension of divine wisdom is beyond human capability. Solomon said, "All this I tested by wisdom and I said, 'I am determined to be wise'— but this was beyond me. Whatever wisdom may be, it is far off and most profound— who can discover it?"[313]

No man could find wisdom out, but it was the Father's good pleasure to reveal His Son. In Christ, we have been given all of God's riches. Now "*it is the Glory of God to conceal a matter; to search out a matter is the glory of kings.*"[314]

In the New Testament, the word "mystery" is used almost exclusively in a sense that the mysteries of God have already been *revealed* in Christ.

Wisdom has already dug deep into the Earth, in order to recover us. And we have been plunged deep into the

---

[312] Job 28:12-15, 20-23, NIV

[313] Eccles. 7:23-24, NIV

[314] Prov. 25:2, NIV

mountain to discover His treasuries. We have been tucked away into the cleft of the rock, which are the very wounds in the body of our Lord. And there we now ask Him to *show us His Glory*. For *in Him are hid all the treasures of wisdom and knowledge.*[315]

[315] See Col. 2:3

+ CHAPTER FIVE
COUNSEL & MIGHT

We now turn to the paired branches of the Spirit of Counsel and Might. Might (or *power*) works together with Counsel in a dynamic way. Flowing together in these two unctions is the ticket for walking in miracles, signs and wonders on a regular basis.

Before we even begin to define these two virtues, I want you to understand that *counsel releases might*. Whenever God counsels us to say, pray or do a thing, you can rest assured that He will follow it up with power. Counsel is simply advice, instruction, guidance or directive leading from God. Many, many people have received prophetic words or directives from God. But not everyone steps into those words or acts on them. Many people have reams of notebooks at home, full of prophetic words, visions and dreams – yet they never took a step of faith to move into those words. Whenever a person acts on counsel, God fulfills the word with power.

In our healing meetings, I have learned over the years to operate comfortably in counsel and might. If God whispers a word or a thought into my mind about a certain sickness – for instance a *deaf right ear* – then I know to act on the word. I either call out the word, lay hands on the person, or simply proclaim that the healing is taking place. It doesn't always matter what I do, as long as I have faith to believe the word of counsel that was given to me.

When I believe the counsel enough to act on it, God always responds with mighty miracle power. He responds not to my actions, but my faith. To this day, we have seen cancers fall off bodies, dozens of deaf ears open, blind eyes open and tumors disappear. We have seen God create gold, silver and new white teeth in people's mouths. We have watched as metal pins, plates and rods have disappeared from bodies. We regularly see weight-loss miracles take place, where people lose fifteen, thirty at times even up to eighty pounds supernaturally! It is amazing to see God move in power. But it usually happens by responding to counsel.

The next time you are in the grocery store, pay attention to the counsel of God. If you hear God tell you to pray for someone in a wheelchair, don't just file the prophetic word away. By faith, you should act on it. By following counsel will you see a miracle of might take place. Might is the manifestation of God's power. It is miracle-working power. It is His *dunamis* or *kratos* power that makes invisible realities pop into the natural realm. The Spirit of Might is miracle oil.

+ Revival at Wal-Mart

A young man from Wisconsin named Ethan recently attended one of our meetings, as I was talking about getting inebriated in the Presence of God and working miracles in Wal-Mart. Ethan was a teenager, and had never done anything like this before. So he decided to take a stroll into Wal-Mart on his own and see what the Lord would do for him.

That night, Ethan led a few people to the Lord. Most Christians would be quite satisfied with an evening like that! But as Ethan drove home, he was frustrated. He had wanted much more. He had big expectancies for a full-fledged outbreak of the Glory in Wal-Mart. As he was driving, the Lord spoke to Ethan and asked him: *What did you want to see?* Ethan thought about it for a moment and told the Lord, "Well, I've never pulled anyone out of a wheelchair before."

The Lord counseled Ethan to return to the store. Ethan turned around and went back to Wal-Mart. He was not finished there. He walked in and went to the automotive aisle of the store. There, he dropped to his knees and began praying. In a few moments, guess what came rolling right in front of him? *A lady in a wheelchair.*

The lady had been in a severe auto accident and was completely paralyzed from the chest down. In fact, her rib cage had been crushed and was wired back together. Ethan began to pray for her. He said that suddenly, it was as if he knew a plethora of healing scriptures by heart – scriptures he had never remembered even reading, yet they came to his lips as he spoke them over her. In a few moments, the woman became amazed. Her toes began to wiggle! Ethan continued to pray. Then came another strange sign – she had *feeling* in the side of her leg which was paralyzed only moments before.

Ethan asked her if she had the faith to step out of the chair. The woman hesitated, but Ethan said, "I do."

He snatched the woman right out of the chair. She took a couple of stammering steps forward, and then … suddenly she began to bolt down the aisle! The woman started jumping and dancing – darting around and screaming through Wal-Mart. By now, a large crowd had begun to gather, gawking at what was happening. Ethan, a teenager with no formal ministry training or seminary credentials, led forty people Jesus that night in Wal-Mart on the heels of this one fantastic miracle.

The Lord had counseled Ethan in the car, and Ethan responded. This enabled the Lord to release His mighty hand of power.

+ The Spirit of Counsel

Counsel always implies advisement from external sources. Counsel, or *`etsah*, refers to instruction that is *given or received* from outside oneself. It is, in its basic form, advice or advisement in plans or direction.

> *Where there is no counsel, the people fall; but in the multitude of counselors there is safety.*[316]

> *Without counsel, plans go awry, but in the multitude of counselors they are established.*[317]

By no means is counsel relegated to healing meetings or receiving words of knowledge. In fact, that is only a single, minor facet of the operation of counsel which I used for demonstration purposes – so you would see its connection with the Spirit of Might. Counsel is far more comprehensive. God wants to instruct you each and every day, in every area of your life. Moreover, He wants you to equip and counsel other people as well. Listening to counsel will bring wisdom to you.[318] And counselors of peace have joy.[319]

---

[316] Prov. 11:14, NKJV
[317] Prov. 15:22, NKJV
[318] See Prov. 19:20
[319] See Prov. 12:20

One of the Lord's names is *Wonderful Counselor,* and interestingly, *Mighty God* is the following title.[320] Holy Spirit is also called the *Counselor*, because He leads us into all truth. Receiving counsel opens up the plans and purposes of God for our lives. Counsel is the directive flow of God that brings you into your destiny. God has predetermined all your steps, and as you heed His counsel, it leads you into the paths of blessing He has in store for you. We never want to forge ahead without the counsel of the Lord. Unlike many wicked kings, David constantly sought the Lord's counsel before he would advance or go to war. God established Him through divine direction, so that David did not make mistakes.

> *Plans are established by counsel; by wise counsel wage war.*[321]

The scriptures encourage us to *wait for counsel.* Do not be headstrong in your own plans. Counsel can be defined as "the power to form wise plans." Might, on the other hand, is the ability to carry those plans into execution. "With men we often find a divorce between the skill to plan and the power to execute," writes one commentator.[322]

If we are not sensitive to Holy Spirit's leading as Counselor, we not only miss a revelation of His plans for us, but we also exclude ourselves from the might afforded to accomplish those plans. God will always call you into things that are impossible for you to achieve. He

---

[320] See Isa. 9:6

[321] Prov. 20:18, NKJV

[322] Spence and Exell, ed., *The Pulpit Commentary: Isaiah*, Vol. 1.

always makes it a requirement for you to trust in His higher abilities than your own inferior ones. Never dismiss counsel, simply because its mandate seems absurdly impossible.

> *However, when He, the Spirit of truth, has come, He will guide you into all truth; for He will not speak on His own authority, but whatever He hears He will speak; and He will tell you things to come. He will glorify Me, for He will take of what is Mine and declare it to you.*[323]

+ Heavenly Councils

You may not realize that there are actually *councils in Heaven.* Not only so, but God brings certain individuals there at times, in order to deliberate over His movements in the Earth. God rarely makes a major move on the Earth without consulting His saints, to whom He delegates authority. Did you know that major issues are decided in these councils, such as: *Should Iraq should be bombed this year? Or who should become the president?* If this sounds far fetched, please read on. …

In the 1960s, during the cold war, our friend John Sandford was first carried into these councils in what began as a visionary experience. John was one of the primary forerunners in the modern prophetic movement of today – if anyone carries the Spirit of Counsel it is John. He pioneered what became the base model for just about every Spirit-filled counseling curriculum today.

---

[323] John 16:13-14, NKJV

You may remember that John the Revelator *interacted* with heavenly beings while in a trance on the Lord's Day.[324] In a similar manner, John Sandford was afforded an opportunity to participate in interactive decision-making in Heaven.

John was with a fellow prophet, when the two were simultaneously taken up. They entered a large chamber and were seated in a circular manner with several others. The Lord then asked them straightforwardly: *Shall we bomb?*

"In those days atomic warfare loomed on the horizon of most people's minds. My friend and I knew we were being asked, in the tremendous economy of words in such councils, whether the time had come to take drastic action. Should God let judgment fall, or would He extend mercy and more time?" writes Sandford.[325]

The council deliberated for a moment, then they asked the Lord, *please give the world more time.*

Instantly, the Lord showed them visions of what would happen if He gave the Earth more time. He saw millions of abortions, homosexuality spreading into government, massacres in Rwanda and Yugoslavia, wars throughout the Earth, escalating divorce rates, bestiality and all manner of sexual perversion and crime. This all flashed before his eyes in a moment, and he knew that these evils would continue to escalate in the Earth if judgment was averted.

---

[324] See Rev. 1

[325] John Loren Sandford, *Healing the Nations: A Call to Global Intercession* (Grand Rapids: Chosen Books, 2000), 138.

Sandford and the others thought about the question once more. Acknowledging that they didn't fully understand what they were asking, they said nevertheless Lord, *give us more time.*

The encounter ended. In just a few short weeks, the world came closer than it had ever been to the very brink of nuclear war. The Cuban missile crisis rose unexpectedly to the surface of world affairs. We may think of those days as an insignificant blip in history. But it was the nearest anyone has ever come to getting their fingerprints on the big red button.

John had been instructed to pray, and as history tells us, the danger soon dissolved away.

+ Changing God's Mind

After reading the preceding story, some might ask: *why would God need advisors*?

It is not so much that God *needs* our advice, as much as He *enjoys* our participation in His activities. Moses was a man who offered counsel to God, and he provoked God to change His mind.[326]

Interestingly, the Bible also tells us that Moses was *more humble than anyone else on the face of the Earth*, and continually sat under the counsel of God in the Tent of Meeting.[327] Did you know that God is the most humble of all? It takes a lot of humility to step down from the glorious splendor of Heaven in order to be birthed

---

[326] See Exod. 32:14

[327] See Num. 12:3

in a manger. God is so humble, that He is willing to receive counsel from men. *He who heeds counsel is wise.*[328] He would not tell us to receive counsel if He is not willing to receive it Himself.

This is the key: God wants you to be so full of His Spirit of Counsel, that He can ask you a question knowing He will receive a good answer. He doesn't want robots, but participatory friends in the Kingdom, who share His throne and authority. He wants to include us in everything. He says of His friend Abraham:

> *Shall I hide from Abraham what I am about to do?*[329]

On the one hand, you are *less than a robot*, in light of God's utter sovereignty! And on the other hand, you are so infused with His divine nature that you are literally a God-communer.

Unlike some churches and secular governments, God does not want a "puppet" elder board who rubber stamp everything at face value. Consider Abraham, who bargained with God over the destruction of Sodom.[330] Of course, the Lord is omniscient and does not need our assistance. But neither is He an insecure leader who is unable to delegate authority. The Lord has delegated the entire Earth to us. Like a good Father who owns the whole house, He still honors the "personal space" of His child's bedroom.

---

[328] See Prov. 12:15

[329] Gen. 18:17, NIV

[330] See Gen. 18

The highest heavens belong to the Lord, but the Earth He has given to man.[331]

This does not mean we must strive again to ascend the ladder of self-works and try to run the world on our own will power! Rather, it means we get to participate in the divine adventure, with the security of knowing He holds the ultimate reins.

At the end of the day, it was not really about Moses' ability to change the mind of God. He was just a foreshadow of the Messiah, who alone would turn the wrath of God away from sinful humanity.

+ Friendly Tent of Counsel

Moses met with God *face to face clearly* in a tent.[332] He was not the only man afforded such a privilege. Another was Job.

Most people think of the life of Job as one of grueling suffering and continual depression. Those people do not understand Job. He was a man who was highly blessed among all his contemporaries. There was a sharp but short window of suffering that came into his life. This lasted but a sliver of time, and then it was immediately followed by a double blessing, greater than everything Job had known before.

Job represents a life of *favor*.

---

331 Ps. 115:16, NIV

332 See Num. 12:8

Consider this passage as Job reminisces back on the good old days, before his present tragedy. These were the days of his prime:

> *Oh, that I were as in months past, as in the days when God watched over me; when* ***His lamp shone upon my head****, and when by His light I walked through darkness; just as I was in the days of my prime,* ***when the friendly counsel of God was over my tent****; when the Almighty was yet with me, when my children were around me; when my steps were bathed with cream (butter), and the rock poured out rivers of oil for me!*
>
> *When I went out to the gate by the city, when I took my seat in the open square, the young men saw me and hid, and the aged arose and stood; the princes refrained from talking, and put their hand on their mouth; the voice of nobles was hushed, and their tongue stuck to the roof of their mouth. When the ear heard, then it blessed me, and when the eye saw, then it approved me. ...*[333]

I believe that the lamp shining over Job's head was the very same Spirit of Counsel that rested over his tent. Because of God's continual counsel, He perpetually favored Job. We read that this blessing kept Job's children around him. He had favor in the marketplace, favor with all generations, favor with politicians and approval from just about everyone. He always had breakthrough, and there were no dry times. Even the hard, rocky places *poured out rivers of oil!*

---

[333] Job 29:2-11, NKJV

The butter on Job's path represents *favor*. One moment of favor with God is worth more than a lifetime of self-effort. The anointing oil of counsel is connected to this buttery path. There is an ease on everything you do, because God directs you. You will expect the best parking spots. You will always get first class upgrades. You will meet just the right people and make just the right connections. There is no friction on your course. When God counsels you, you move only where He guides you, and you slip and slide right along effortlessly in His buttery grace.

Understand that this is not counsel for just one specific circumstance. Not counsel that comes on a case-by-case basis. Rather, this is a continual wellspring of counsel – the Spirit of Counsel is an unending cloud of direction that lingers over you. It is like the cloud that led the Israelites in the desert. This is *friendly* counsel, and it sits on you both day and night. Often the Lord speaks to me this way as I lie in bed at night or in the early morning hours.

> *I will bless the Lord who has given me counsel; my heart also instructs me in the night seasons. I have set the Lord always before me; because He is at my right hand I shall not be moved.*[334]

There is one more ingredient here. Remember that counsel must be *followed*, in order for the power and favor to follow. You will notice that Job did not merely follow the counsel that *benefitted him*. He followed the whole counsel of God – and that included constantly thinking of others. The benefits of God's absolute

---

[334] Ps. 16:7-8, NKJV

power will only follow those who absolutely follow His counsel.

Job qualifies this description of his favored lifestyle. He continues to tell us *why* there was so much butter on His life. The reason he walked in such extravagance was explicitly linked to his obedience in caring for the poor, the orphan, the widow, the oppressed and the disenfranchised:

> *Because I delivered the poor who cried out, the fatherless and the one who had no helper. The blessing of a perishing man came upon me, and I caused the widow's heart to sing for joy. I put on righteousness, and it clothed me; my justice was like a robe and a turban. I was eyes to the blind, and I was feet to the lame. I was a father to the poor, and I searched out the case that I did not know. I broke the fangs of the wicked, and plucked the victim from his teeth.*[335]

If you are seeking the counsel of God on a directional matter in your life, never get so caught up in the specifics of your own situation that you selfishly forget about others. Don't neglect the poor. Think outside yourself. It's liberating!

Likewise, if you need advice on a matter, never forget the bigger picture of His Word. The Bible is full of general counsel that applies to us. Don't forget to honor your parents. Follow the Ten Commandments. How often do I meet a person who needs a word from the

---

[335] Job 29:12-17, NKJV

Lord, but they aren't following the sixty-six chapters of words they already have!

The Bible never says that God specifically told Job to take care of the poor. I don't think it was a *specific mandate* just for him. He seemed to understand that this was the counsel of God for all of mankind – stuff everybody should be doing – and so he walked in it. All of us are called to share the gospel with the lost. All of us are instructed to give tithes and offerings. These are general principles of counsel that, when followed, will bring blessings to our lives.

I'm not giving you formulas to favor. God has no favorites. He pours favor freely to all, and counsel freely to all who simply listen. The crazy thing about the gospel is that He even empowers and works through us so that it is *Him* obeying the Word through us. That's where the butter freely flows.

+ The Spirit of Power

Counsel without might is talk without power. Power is not simply the splitting of the Red Sea or the healing of blind eyes. Meekness is power under control. The humility of the great saints, or their longsuffering, also speaks of great depths of power. Nevertheless, words must eventually bear action and fruit.

> *For the Kingdom of God is not a matter of talk but of power.*[336]

---

336 1 Cor. 4:20, NIV

The Spirit of Might concerns supernatural manifestations of power in the Earth. Furthermore, the apostle Paul said, "My message and my preaching were not with wise and persuasive words, but with a demonstration of the Spirit's power."[337] It is this vein of the Spirit's sevenfold function that most pertains to the phenomenal – the working of marvels.

A classic example of the Spirit of Might coming upon a person is found in the Old Testament example of Samson. In numerous passages, we read that the Lord would *come upon him in power*. For example:

> *Samson went down to Timnah together with his father and mother. As they approached the vineyards of Timnah, suddenly a young lion came roaring toward him. The Spirit of the Lord came upon him in power so that he tore the lion apart with his bare hands as he might have torn a young goat.*[338]

This demonstration of strength did not come from natural or jiu-jitsu skills! The Spirit of Might supernaturally enabled Samson, so that he could rip apart a lion. This is not a make-believe story. This was a clothing of strength that came upon him. David, still in his youth – likely before twelve years of age – had two similar instances just like this one. As a youngster, David killed both a bear and a lion, seizing them in hand-to-hand combat.[339] This is not normal behavior for an adolescent boy.

---

[337] 1 Cor. 2:4, NIV

[338] Judg. 14:5-6, NIV

[339] 1 Sam. 17:34-37

Consider a time later in life, when David had amassed his *mighty men* around him. David's mighty men were so called because they operated in the Spirit of Might. These were no less than super-heroes of old. Yet little attention is paid to them, perhaps because scholars think them more the fodder of Sunday school fairy tales than real men.

+ THE MIGHTY MEN

David had two tiers of Mighty Men. There were the *Thirty*, and then there were the *Three*. You were no sissy if you were counted among the Thirty. But if you were among the Three, it is doubtless everyone gladly gave you the VIP lane everywhere you went! Consider how dynamically invincible were these renowned men:

> *Josheb-Basshebeth, a Tahkemonite, was chief of the Three; he raised his spear against eight hundred men, whom he killed in one encounter.*[340]

Do you realize that you cannot simply kill eight hundred men in one sitting simply from working out at the gym? This was not physical strength that empowered the mighty men, but a divine reckoning was released via the Spirit of Might. Consequently, Josheb here was the strongest man in the army, and his name meant "dwelling in rest." The power of God is often summed up in a still, small voice. It is the God of Peace who crushes satan under our feet.

Consider the second of the Three. His name was Eleazar. All of his fellow soldiers deserted him in the

---

[340] 2 Sam. 23:8, NIV

middle of a fight amongst the Philistines, but Eleazar stood his ground "and struck down the Philistines till his hand grew tired and froze to the sword. The Lord brought about a great victory that day. The troops returned to Eleazar, but only to strip the dead."[341]

These men must have possessed a veritable force field of power emanating from their bodies. To watch them engaged in battle probably looked more like a modern science fiction movie than real live warfare. It seems that many carried this same Spirit, as we read of a whole group of Gadite army commanders of whom "the least was a match for a hundred, and the greatest for a thousand."[342]

In one sweeping rage, the Spirit of the Lord came upon Samson *in powe*r and he killed one thousand Philistines with the jawbone of a donkey.[343] It wipes me out to lay hands on a thousand people to pray for them. I go tennis elbow from hugging over a thousand people once! I could not imagine the well of divine energy it must have required for such a brutal task. After this mighty feat, Samson was nearly dying of thirst, and the Lord miraculously opened a spring of water for him from the ground. This too was the Spirit of Might at work. All miracles are the jurisdiction of the Spirit of Might. I simply use these stories of natural warfare to highlight the superhuman abilities one has under its influence. Obviously as Christians, we do not wage war as the world does. Our warfare employs spiritual weaponry,

---

[341] 2 Sam. 23:10, NIV

[342] See 1 Chron. 12:14

[343] See Judg. 15:15

but those weapons are mighty – they have the power of God to pull down strongholds.[344]

In the latter rains of God's Glory on the Earth, one individual will be like many mighty men put together.[345] David was not supposed to count his armies, because their strength was not in numbers. It was in the Lord. Those men were literally fighting over bean fields, but now we are establishing the very Kingdom of God.

Scripture is full of fantastic wonders that boggle the mind – miracles that cannot merely be classified into theological categories. Elijah outran a chariot after calling down fire from the sky and killing 450 prophets of Baal. Gideon's three hundred men destroyed an army of 135,000 – likewise an odds of 450 to one. The Spirit of Might multiplies your power. It brings mystical abilities for the working of miracles. Church history is chock full of saints who floated off the ground in ecstasy, raised dead bodies from a decayed skeletal condition or parted bodies of water. Men have communicated with animals, such as St. Francis of Assisi, while others have physically transported from one place to another. In my previous two books, *The New Mystics* and *The Ecstasy of Loving God*, I have provided an extensive amount of supernatural church history. The miraculous is as familiar to the life of the church as it was to the canon of scripture. The Spirit of Might affects each and every miracle.

As a believer, you can be clothed continually in this anointing.

---

[344] See 2 Cor. 10:3-4

[345] See Zech. 10:5

+ The Saint who Moved a Mountain

Faith is truly a prerequisite for operating in the Spirit of Might. Simon the Tanner was an ascetic man who lived in north Egypt in the late tenth century. At that time, the secular ruler, Fatimid Caliph Al-Muizz Li-Deenillah, was accustomed to hosting amicable debates between leading Christian, Jewish and Muslim leaders. One day, after a Christian leader gained an upper hand in his assertions for the faith, his Jewish antagonist posed a challenge. He quoted from the very words of Jesus in the Christian scriptures:

> *I tell you the truth, if you have faith as small as a mustard seed, you can say to this mountain, "Move from here to there" and it will move. Nothing will be impossible for you.*[346]

This verse, said the Jewish debater, was the litmus test as to whether Christianity is valid. The Caliph was a shrewd politician, and he saw an opportunity for ridding himself of the Christians. The Caliph instructed the Christian leaders to move Mokattam Mountain. If they could not do it, this would be proof positive that Christianity is wrong, and he would completely do away with them all. They would be forced to convert to islam, leave Egypt or be killed.

Of course this was quite the predicament for church leaders at the time. They were given only three days to make it happen. After a period of prayer, they felt led to call on Simon the Tanner, a poor monastic type who cared for the poor and lived a solitary life. Having gath-

---

[346] Matt. 17:20, NIV

ered the local believers at the mountain for prayer, eyewitnesses report that the Simon instructed leaders on how to pray and what to do. There, in the presence of the Caliph, Mokattam Mountain heaved and lifted from its base in such a way that sunlight could be seen underneath it.

Completely shell shocked, the Caliph offered the church anything they wanted. He eventually became baptized, and his baptismal pool is still on display in Egypt today. Today, there is also a massive Coptic Christian church that meets at the base of Mokattam Mountain, the site of this tremendous miracle.[347]

Counsel released the Spirit of Might.

+ Resurrection Power

The Spirit of Power is very comprehensive in what it can accomplish. One believer can essentially do anything, according to scripture, as "all things are possible to him who believes."[348] Besides miracles, the power of God working through us provides boldness for witness. In Acts 2, we see Peter boldly preaching, accusing thousands of Jews for their murder of Jesus on Pentecost. But only a few days earlier, he was so afraid of one young servant girl that he denied the Lord.[349]

The Spirit of Might is a vigorously emboldening infusion of authority. The Psalmist speaks of our horn of

---

347 Visit www.cavechurch.com as a source from the actual church that meets at this site today. Also more history on Simon can be found at http://orthodoxwiki.org/Simon_the_Shoemaker.

348 See Mark 9:23

349 See Matt. 26

authority when the oil of the Spirit of Might comes upon us:

> *You have exalted my horn like that of a wild ox; fine oils have been poured upon me.*[350]

Your inner strength and authority brings an aggressive boldness to confront sin structures, as the prophet Micah said, "as for me, I am filled with power, with the Spirit of the Lord, and with justice and might, to declare to Jacob his transgression, to Israel his sin."[351] But moreover, it is the power of love, that many waters cannot quench – a love unyielding as the grave.

This might does not simply come upon a believer, but runs through your veins like a never-ending river. It is resurrection power that indwells you:

> *And if the Spirit of Him who raised Jesus from the dead is living in you, He who raised Christ from the dead will also give life to your mortal bodies through His Spirit, who lives in you.*[352]

Paul the apostle further explains to us about "His incomparably great power for us who believe. That power is like the working of His mighty strength, which He exerted in Christ when He raised Him from the dead and seated Him at His right hand in the heavenly realms."[353]

---

[350] Ps. 92:10, NIV

[351] Mic. 3:8, NIV

[352] Rom. 8:11, NIV

[353] Eph. 1:19-20, NIV

So you see this power within you is not merely something that raises a dead body, but also the same power that glorifies that body and seats you in eternal realms of glorious authority. It is the very *same essence* of God that quickened Jesus in His entire earthly ministry. The physical body of Jesus was taken back up to Heaven. But now, you are His body here on the Earth. You are the container of His Spirit in this world. This is why He tells us in John 14:12 that, "I can guarantee this truth: Those who believe in me will do the things that I am doing. They will do even greater things because I am going to the Father."[354]

Each of us is anointed with the same power, the same sevenfold virtue that rested on Christ. When Jesus breathed on His disciples saying, "receive the Holy Spirit," He also assured them that, "As the Father has sent me, I am sending you."[355] How did the Father send Jesus? *God anointed Jesus of Nazareth with the Holy Spirit and with power.*[356] You are anointed no differently than the Christ was anointed. It is His oil that has smeared you. Trust in it. Walk like it.

+ KRATOS

There are a number of words for "power" in the New Testament. These primarily include *kratos*, *dunamis, ischys and energeia/energeo*.

---

[354] John 14:12, GWT

[355] John 20:21-22, NIV

[356] Acts 10:38, NIV

Kratos is *dominion* power.[357] Throughout the New Testament, it is used in territorial or provincial reference to the absolute authority of the Lord Jesus. It is the type of power related to mastery or victory in war. There are many verses which concern the dominion of Christ, and that dominion resides within the believer.[358] Kratos is related to His kingship and His enthroned power. It is the place of positional control over everything, from which the outworking of other supernatural abilities flow.

> *Finally, my brethren, be strong in the Lord, and in the power (kratos) of His might.*[359]

Kratos power in the inner man enables *dunamis*, which is active power for the working of miracles, as well as the ability to bear good character and fruit of the Spirit.

> *Strengthened with all might, according to His glorious power (kratos), unto all patience and longsuffering with joyfulness.*[360]

+ DUNAMIS

Dunamis is strength, power or ability, but specifically it is "inherent power, power residing in a thing by virtue of its nature, or which a person or thing exerts and puts

---

[357] Strong, *Exhaustive Concordance of the Bible*, Entry 2904.
[358] See 1 Pet. 4:11; 1 Pet. 5:11; Jude 1:25; 1 Tim. 6:16; Rev. 1:6; Rev. 5:13
[359] Eph. 6:10, KJV
[360] Col. 1:11, KJV

forth. … Power for performing miracles. … Moral power and excellence of soul."[361]

Dunamis, or *dynamis*, is the same root word for the English term "dynamite." It was by far the favorite term employed in the Pauline epistles to describe the power of God. This is also the power exerted by Jesus in the gospels in the working of miracles, and is often translated as "mighty works." This would include healing the sick, raising the dead and casting out devils.

> *And when He had called His twelve disciples to Him, He gave them power (dunamis) over unclean spirits, to cast them out, and to heal all kinds of sickness and all kinds of disease.*[362]

Furthermore, we see that the disciples later in the chapter exerted this very dunamis:

> *And as you go, preach, saying, "The Kingdom of Heaven is at hand." Heal the sick, cleanse the lepers, raise the dead, cast out demons. Freely you have received, freely give.*[363]

Dunamis is the all-purpose power of God that comes upon the believer with the baptism of Holy Spirit. It is the equipping, enabling power given for witnessing to the Lordship of Christ. It is the word used in this familiar passage:

---

[361] Strong, *Exhaustive Concordance of the Bible*, Entry 1411.

[362] Matt. 10:1, NKJV

[363] Matt. 10:7-8, NKJV

But you shall receive power (ability, efficiency, and might) when the Holy Spirit has come upon you, and you shall be My witnesses in Jerusalem and all Judea and Samaria and to the ends (the very bounds) of the Earth.[364]

Perhaps William Vine gives us the clearest, most concise definition of *dunamis* as "power in action."[365]

Remember that dunamis is also interconnected and, at times, used synonymously with kratos, ischys and energeia. Ischys is a simple, general word that refers to "strength that is possessed." It may refer to the natural strength of a man, or the strength of God. Kratos, however, to the Greek mind symbolizes something more profound. Kratos was the name of their *god of strength* in mythology. The authority of the believer in the working of miracles, hinges ultimately on the overarching kratos Kingdom dominion he has in Christ. This lordship authority activates the hands-on dunamis. See how the two work together:

And what is the exceeding greatness of His power (dunamis) to us-ward who believe, according to the working of His mighty power (kratos).[366]

This can literally be translated "according to the power of the power of His power."[367] There are three words for power used in this verse. Besides kratos and duna-

---

[364] Acts 1:8, AMP

[365] W.E. Vine, *Expository Dictionary of New Testament Words*, 1940 (Accessible online at www.antioch.com.sg/bible/vines).

[366] Eph. 1:19, KJV notes mine

[367] Darrell Bock, *The Bible Knowledge Word Study* (Colorado Springs, CO: Cook Communications Ministries, 2006), 429.

mis, there is also the word from which we get the English term *energy*. It is *energeia* which comes from *energos.*[368] According to a number of Greek scholars, *energeia* is almost exclusively active, effectual, *operative* power. Think of it as the actual lightning bolts by which dunamis operates! The Spirit of Might is the actual energy of God flowing through you!

Because of the positional dominion of Christ, He expects all of us to operate in dunamis. There is no excuse for powerless Christianity. Dunamis is not relegated to special "miracle workers." Jesus had a beef with the Sadducees over this very issue. They claimed to have a command over the word of God, but they didn't even recognize God's messenger. Likewise, they did not know His power.

> *Jesus answered and said unto them, Ye do err, not knowing the scriptures, nor the power of God (dunamis).*[369]

Jesus is our perfect model for flowing in power *continually*. You have billions of potential volts of power latent inside of you, which can be released at all times by faith. The Spirit of Might is not merely "getting lucky" sometimes when you pray for a sick person. It is not a one-time miracle, but the continuous Spirit of miracle-working power. Jesus healed *everyone*, except in those rare occasions when their own hardness of heart isolated people from God. See how the anointing operated in His life: *God anointed Jesus of Nazareth*

---

[368] Strong, *Exhaustive Concordance of the Bible*, See entries 1753 and 1756.

[369] Matt. 22:29, KJV

with the Holy Spirit and with power, and because God was with Him, He went around doing good and healing everyone who was oppressed by the devil."[370]

Dunamis flowed out of Jesus like a tangible, quantifiable substance. It was always present, because Holy Spirit came upon Him and remained.[371] When the woman pressed through the crowd to touch the hem of Jesus' garment, the *virtue* which flowed out of Him was actually "dunamis."

> *And Jesus, immediately knowing in Himself that virtue (dunamis) had gone out of Him, turned Him about in the press, and said, who touched my clothes?*[372]

Besides the explicitly "supernatural" aspect of dunamis, everyone is endowed with natural abilities or talents that are from God. Whether artistic or mathematic skill, business acumen or an eye for antiques, God *empowers* us with these talents. Though we may not consider these talents to be *supernatural*, they still originate from the life breath of His Spirit. Consider the parable of the talents:

> *And unto one he gave five talents, to another two, and to another one; to every man according to his several ability (dunamis). ...*[373]

---

370 Acts 10:38, ISV

371 See John 1:33

372 Mark 5:30, KJV

373 Matt. 25:15, KJV

While man is quickened with divine ability, the Spirit of Might is far more than mere natural strength. Ecclesiastes 9:16 says, "Wisdom is better than strength." Natural strength is limited and temporal, but the very power of God is inexhaustible.

+ THE ENERGY OF GOD

Energeia is used eight times in the New Testament, as well as *energeo* always referring to supernatural energy. Once it is used in reference to satanic energy. The apostle Paul uses the word *energy* "to refer to the actualization of power in concrete circumstances," write Hawthorne, Martin and Reid in their *Dictionary of Paul and His Letters*. "He often has in mind the supernatural power of the Spirit. Similarly, his use of the expressions 'grace,' 'glory,' 'fullness' and even 'in Christ' often convey the notion of divine power as part of their contextual meanings."[374]

Again, dunamis is not relegated specifically to physical healings, but is involved in any type of supernatural or creative miracle. When Holy Spirit came upon Mary to give birth to Jesus, the angel said, "The power (dunamis) of the Highest shall overshadow thee."[375]

Of all the sevenfold, the Spirit of Might is specifically the most tangible, visible or naturally manifest flow of Holy Spirit. Might is the Spirit that births realities from the invisible realm into the visible realm. It is the Spirit of awe and wonder, miracles and signs. The Spirit of

---

[374] Hawthorne, Martin and Reid, ed., *Dictionary of Paul and His Letters*, 723.
[375] Luke 1:35, KJV

Might always concerns the *manifestation* or delivery of the Kingdom into the physical, natural world. You can see, hear, touch, smell or taste the effects of might. It always physically demonstrates Heaven on Earth.

Just as the Spirit of Might enabled Christ to manifest as a child in the Earth, so does the Spirit of Might want to birth a fresh expression of Jesus in your own life and calling.

+ THE ULTIMATE POWER

The apostle Paul always reminds us that the cross was the ultimate representation of the power of God. It is the source of the believer's power in every area. Among other things, let's look at the cross as 1) the power to save; 2) the power against evil; and 3) the power to love and serve.

The gospel is the "dunamis of God for the salvation of everyone who believes."[376] Jesus came to demonstrate the comprehensive might of God, of which miracle-working power is only a small, minute portion. Paul noted that the Jews sought miraculous signs, but that he preached "Christ crucified. ... Christ is the power of God."[377] The apparent weakness of Christ on the cross is in actuality the very power of God.

As the *power to save*, the cross liberates us from the bondage to sin, sickness, poverty and every enslavement of the world. Through Christ, mankind was liber-

---

[376] See Rom. 1:16; 1 Cor. 1:18

[377] See 1 Cor. 1:22-24

ated from decay. He is released from death, the corruption of the flesh and the law.

As the *power against evil*, the cross overcomes every demonic supernatural force arrayed against the church. Used as a general word for *power*, we see that angelic and demonic hosts operate in Godly or ungodly dunamis. Jesus spoke of the stars falling from heaven and that the "*dunamis of the heavens shall be shaken.*"[378]

Angels are constantly interacting on the Earth to release the dunamis of God in favor of believers, just as satan operates in illegal power. However, all the power of the enemy, including those "principalities and powers" of Ephesians 6 have been utterly defeated in one fell swoop on the cross. The enemy is rendered impotent and his power useless against the one who trusts that the work of the cross has finished him once and for all.

Your efforts, intercession and ability to believe will never be the antidote to the evil. The shed blood of Christ has overcome evil. All was accomplished through His efforts, His intercession and His grace that *enables* you to believe. All three adversaries of the church – satan, the flesh and the world – were finally and completely eradicated on the cross.

> *May I never boast except in the cross of our Lord Jesus Christ, through which the world has been crucified to me, and I to the world.*[379]

---

[378] See Matt. 24:29

[379] Gal. 6:14, NIV

As the *power to serve*, the work of the cross now enables us to do the work of the Kingdom supernaturally in the capacity of our new creation realities. Like Paul, we can labor super-humanly, "with all the energy and power of Christ at work in me."[380] We can serve in ways that are necessarily beyond the old Adamic ability, because we are not simply *new Adams*. We are no longer human in respect to what we once were. We are new creations in type and quality. Sons and daughters of God. It is not out of our own human ability that we operate any longer. Paul said, "when I am weak, then I am strong!"[381] The ability, or quickening of God, is the grace that now animates our bodily members, because we mystically died on the cross. Now we no longer live, but Christ lives in us![382]

The Spirit of Might now infuses you with divine ability in every imaginable area. While we have covered the Greek words for might, it is worthwhile to note the original Hebrew word for the Spirit of Might in Isaiah 11:2 is *gebuwrah*.[383] Its meaning is synonymous with its Greek counterparts: *valor, victory, force, mastery, vigor*. But most interesting is that this is actually a *feminine* word! It has been said that, "hell hath no fury like a woman scorned." Surely this is true when we consider the *warrior bride* of Christ!

---

[380] Col. 1:28-29, NEB

[381] See 2 Cor. 12:10

[382] See Gal. 2:20

[383] Strong, *Exhaustive Concordance of the Bible*, Entry 1369.

+ Chapter Six
Knowledge & the Fear of the Lord

There is a final pairing on our lampstand as we turn to the two remaining *Spirits of the Lord* listed in the Isaiah 11 pattern. They are the Spirit of Knowledge and the Spirit of the Fear of the Lord. We will see in this chapter how both knowledge and the fear of the Lord are by no means mutually exclusive. On the contrary, they are completely interdependent upon one another in Kingdom operations.

For starters, let us differentiate the Spirit of Knowledge from a mere *word of knowledge.* A word of knowledge is a gift – a piece of factual information that is supernaturally discerned, such as a name, address or true-life prophetic insight. It is one of the nine spiritual gifts listed in 1 Corinthians 12 that comes by revelation, giving you information about an individual, place or situation. However the Spirit of Knowledge is not a gift, but a *person of God.* He is the giver of the factual message. He is the source.

God doesn't give knowledge. *He is knowledge.*

Paul tells the Corinthians, "For I resolved to *know nothing* while I was with you except Jesus Christ and Him crucified."[384]

Some people pray diligently to receive a piece of knowledge – a fact, revelation or insight from God. And God is faithful to give us this information by His grace when a situation merits it. But wouldn't it be far more beneficial to be continually immersed and carried

---

[384] 1 Cor. 2:2, NIV

along by the River of Knowledge? Many people pray and fast and strive to pump up a single drink at the well. They labor to fill their little cup with one revelatory word from God as a situation demands. But instead, what if a river of revelation took you over, overwhelmed you, possessed you, and pulled your feet right off the bank?

+ THE SPIRIT OF KNOWLEDGE

One by one, you can push and pull and strain your ear to hear a word from God on a case-by-case basis. You go into your prayer closet for a week, and finally come up with an answer to your situation. Like pumping up a little cup of water, you can somewhat control and "work" your word of knowledge gift. Because it is a gift, it is like a tool on your tool belt to use at your own whim and pleasure. This is possible because the spirit of a prophet is subject to the prophet.[385] But it is far superior to allow the river of revelation control you! Instead of just using the gifts on our tool belt, He wants your whole life latched onto *His* tool belt, to be controlled, possessed and used at *His* whim and pleasure. You do not control this river; it controls you. And wherever it flows, there is an abundance of divine knowledge and revelation for every situation you encounter, with no effort or striving of your own. You are living in a continual overflow of God's presence, rather than being gift-focused.

The charismatic movement of the past several decades demanded a need for a reintroduction of the spiritual gifts to the church. For this reason, it was necessary to

---

[385] See 1 Cor. 14:32

teach on the functions of the gifts. But along with any new emphasis the Lord brings to the church will come those who camp at a certain paradigm and miss the bigger picture. In this way, many have become "gifting" focused, with reams of books and teaching materials focused on perfecting prophetic gifts, healing gifts and the like. And amid the thrill of the church being empowered, we often took our eyes off the main thing.

Did Jesus get too boring for us? Why are we peddling with trifles and trinkets that fall from His pockets, when all of the Glory and power of the cosmos are reconciled in this One who is united to us?

To this day, there are numerous believers who measure their own spirituality based on the level at which their prophetic gift has been developed or how many sick people they can heal. What a gross deception. Our spirituality is based no more or less than on the perfect sacrifice of the Son of God. He is no more impressed by your honed prophetic prowess than the fact that you tied your shoes all by yourself this morning.

Praise God for His gift of the word of knowledge, but a word of knowledge is ultimately dictated by the situation. The Spirit of Knowledge, on the other hand, has power to dictate the situation itself.

No longer be mesmerized by words of knowledge. Be mesmerized by the *person of Christ* who is the Spirit of Knowledge.

CHAPTER SIX

+ AN INTIMATE KNOWING

This is a knowledge related to the heart, rather than the head of the believer. This is not mental knowledge, but *intimate* knowledge that we now possess. The word for "knowledge," *da`ath*, can speak of cunning, skill or mental premeditation.[386] But it is not merely factual information – rather it is a perception and awareness of Him.

> *Knowledge puffs up, but love builds up.*[387]

This is an intimate knowing, rather than an intellectual knowing. It is not unlike when a man "knows" a woman in scripture. This same word for *knowing* the Lord is a prerequisite for entering the Kingdom:

> *Many will say to me on that day, "Lord, Lord, did we not prophesy in your name, and in your name drive out demons and perform many miracles?" Then I will tell them plainly, "**I never knew you.** Away from me, you evildoers!"*[388]

The Ronald Knox translation of the New Testament interprets this passage as saying "you were never friends of mine."[389] Religion is the substitution of service or factual information about God in place of a personal, intimate awareness of Him.

---

[386] Strong, *Exhaustive Concordance of the Bible*, Entry 1847.

[387] 1 Cor. 8:1, NIV

[388] Matt. 7:22-23, NIV

[389] Matt. 7:22-23, KNOX

This *knowing* is not a memorization of theological knowledge. Rather it can be deemed an *acknowledgement* of the person of Christ. Consider as Hosea writes:

> *Hear the word of the Lord, you Israelites, because the Lord has a charge to bring against you who live in the land: "There is no faithfulness,* ***no love, no acknowledgment of God*** *in the land."*[390]

The Lord states that He was not pleased with the prophecies, exorcisms or miracle working of those who approached Him on the Day of Judgment. His only pleasure is found in the offering of Christ on Calvary. The fact that these people pointed to their own accomplishments, rather than His, was the very thing that disqualified them for entry. Our acknowledgement of His sacrifice is the only acceptable offering that qualifies us for admission.

Consider Hosea 6:6 in the following three translations in light of our primary need to intimately "acknowledge" Him. This is the Spirit of Knowledge:

> *For I desire mercy, not sacrifice, and* ***acknowledgment of God*** *rather than burnt offerings.*[391]

> *For I delight in loyalty rather than sacrifice, And in the* ***knowledge of God*** *rather than burnt offerings.*[392]

---

[390] Hosea 4:1, NIV

[391] Hosea 6:6, NIV

[392] Hosea 6:6, NASB

I want your loyalty, not your sacrifices. ***I want you to know me****, not to give me burnt offerings.*[393]

Hear the resounding theme? He wants lovers, not mere psychics.

Factual details do come by revelation. The Lord often shows me people's names, allows me to discern their diseases, etc. when I am ministering in meetings. I very regularly know about situations that are happening to friends and relatives, without ever having talked with them about it. But even factual revelations like this should come as a byproduct of *intimate* knowledge. Paul, in praying for prophetic illumination, asked that the *eyes of our hearts* be enlightened. God is not looking for mere fortune tellers who possess clairvoyant knowledge of supernatural facts. He is instead looking for intimate lovers of Him, whose *hearts* have been enlightened – not just their prophetic radars. Such lovers will be privy to an immense wealth of knowledge in the coming days.

Imagine a believer who no longer needs his mobile device, because he is like a living Google internet portal – able to pull up any information at any given time. This could look much like the Boise, Idaho pastor Roland Buck who, in the late 1970s, had revelatory encounters where thousands of verses of scripture were supernaturally infused into his memory. He was like a walking concordance.[394] The Lord wants to entrust such a

---

[393] Hosea 6:6, GWT

[394] For more on Roland Buck, see my earlier book, *The New Mystics* (Shippensburg, PA: Destiny Image Publishers, 2006), 372.

manifestation to friends, not slaves. Those whose hearts are fully His.

It is an age-old heresy to believe we are saved by the accumulation of knowledge itself. This is called gnosticism, from the root word "gnosis," *to know*. Knowledge does not save you, Jesus does. The spiritual life is not a mental ascent, nor is it the attainment of "secret knowledge." This is the deceptive lure of new agers, freemasons, Christian science practitioners and just about every occultic religion on the planet. The stumbling block of the true Gospel is that all its mystery was laid bare on the cross – that it is so simple; even a little child can perceive it. The deepest secrets of Heaven were plainly published on the cross. There is no cloaking, shroud or veil of partition that separates us. No seminary degrees, deeper prophetic insight, or initiation rites are required. Beware the man who complicates this gospel. Woe to him who puts it out of reach from the lowly and the simple.

Every stream of the church has been infected by some degree of gnosticism. For mainline churches, it is the pursuit of theological studies and Bible memorization that somehow "spiritualizes" its adherents. Of course we should know the scriptures, but Jesus said this about such mental ascent:

> *You diligently study the Scriptures because you think that by them you possess eternal life. These are the Scriptures that testify about me, yet you refuse to come to me to have life.*[395]

---

[395] John 5:39-40, NIV

For modern charismatics, there are far crazier examples of gnosticism. Charismatics love to boast in their revelatory insights. Usually it is the flavor of the month variety of spiritual knowledge that most impresses. I will give you an example. ... It is very trendy today among many "cutting edge" prophetic ministers to teach on metaphysics, in an attempt to show parallels between scientific and spiritual principles. They talk about Einstein and atom splitting and sound frequencies and DNA and all manner of elusive scientific principles in a way that makes them to appear more spiritual. I know one guy who claims that God showed him all of Einstein's diagrams in the spirit before he ever studied the scientist's books! This is usually followed by lots of "oohs" and "aahs" by the crowd.

Now let me first say that scientific-to-spiritual parallels are completely valid in their place. There are natural, scientific laws that are held together by scriptural principles. In fact, Isaac Newton and many other scientists framed their observations based on scriptural truths. There is no question that certain metaphysical observations exist which validate spiritual principles. But there is a point where this train begins to derail.

The problem does not lie in the legitimacy of metaphysical analogies to the word of God. Instead, the problem comes from an underlying current which says that by "knowing" more about metaphysical principles (or anything for that matter), that somehow you are going to become more spiritual. You will work better miracles. You will "access the spirit realm," etc. Again, we see that intellectual knowledge subtly becomes the key to a more fulfilling spiritual life. The science book may give you some interesting insights, but at the end of the day Christianity is not algebra class. Don't be intimidated by those who try to "one-up" you with their revelations, no matter how deep or seemingly valid.

There is a very real knowledge that we are always maturing into, and that is the intimate knowledge of the Lord Himself.

> *But grow in the grace and knowledge of our Lord and Savior Jesus Christ. To Him be Glory both now and forever! Amen.*[396]

Always remember that it was the Tree of Knowledge that got Adam and Eve booted from the Garden. There is a sharp contrast between the *knowledge of good and evil* and the knowledge of Him. Prophetic writer Rick Joyner often points out that good and evil have the same root. It is not an awareness of good and evil that makes us spiritual, but rather it is feasting on the other tree in the Garden – the Tree of Life. In his timeless book *There Were Two Trees in the Garden*, Joyner writes, "Satan did not tempt Eve with the fruit of the Tree of Knowledge just because of the Lord's prohibition. He tempted her with it because the source of his power was rooted in that tree. Furthermore, the Lord did not implement this restriction just to test Adam and Eve; He prohibited the eating of its fruit because He knew it was poison."[397]

Knowledge without love is dangerous. Knowledge harnessed by love in the fear of the Lord is a powerful tool.

---

[396] 2 Pet. 3:18, NIV

[397] Rick Joyner, *There Were Two Trees in the Garden* (Springdale, PA: Whitaker House, 1993), 9.

The human intellect is amoral. It can be used either for good or evil, depending on its governing force. In the possession of a madman like Hitler, genius is a tool for destruction. But in the hands of a Solomon, it is a powerful instrument for good. Contrary to the opinion of many believers, intellectualism is not the enemy of faith. Only it must follow faith, not precede it. Greco-rationalism is a terrible governor, but a powerful servant. Here are a few verses touting the benefits of knowledge:

> *... a man of knowledge increases strength.*[398]

> *The heart of him who has understanding seeks knowledge. ...*[399]

> *The lips of the wise disperse knowledge.*[400]

> *... it is not good for a soul to be without knowledge.*[401]

> *Wise people store up knowledge. ...*[402]

We have made the point that the Spirit of Knowledge is primarily oriented toward the intimate knowledge of God. Yet this intimate friendship does translate into a practical hearing of His voice as we live a life continually acquainted with Him. Living in the river of His love will result in a steady stream of God-given knowl-

---

398 Prov. 24:5, NIV
399 Prov. 15:14, NKJV
400 Prov. 15:7, NKJV
401 Prov. 19:2, NKJV
402 Prov. 10:14, NKJV

edge into all manner of subjects. Because of the anointing, the scriptures tell us that we "know all things."[403] We have access to every bit of information we need in the spirit realm. This comes not by the work of study, but by the Spirit of Knowledge. His friends hear His voice.

When the Lord first began giving me words of knowledge, I would know all sorts of things about people – even their secret sins! I would sometimes discern what someone's occupation was – whether they were in the medical field or real estate. I would know something they had experienced in their life – good or bad, recent or past. I began to know the thoughts of people. Sometimes I would be speaking with someone, and *I knew that they knew that I knew* their thoughts! This supernatural ability to know things began to increase, and get more accurate. I remember talking to a friend on the phone in the early days of my Christian walk. As we talked, he was in the kitchen at home looking for something. I told him to look in the dishwasher on the top shelf in the back left corner and he would find what he needed. Sure enough, it was there! Little things like these were faith accelerators.

As I grew in operating in the Spirit of Knowledge, I ceased to "press in" for words anymore. Hearing my Father's voice, I found, was an effortless gift of grace. I simply practiced His presence. Enjoying His nearness, I would simply "know" things without looking for them. I knew when a couple was having trouble in their marriage, even though I was thousands of miles away. I knew when a fellow minister was gossiping about me

---

[403] See 1 John 2:20

even though there were no outward indications he was doing so. I would be aware if employees were slacking off. Corporately, I can regularly "know the thoughts" of the people as I am preaching – just as Jesus discerned the thoughts of the Pharisees while speaking to them in the crowd. Coming into this gift was not a labor, nor was there an intensive spiritual training I underwent, about which I can boast or give you formulas to copy. Words of knowledge flow with ease from the secret place. When you spend time with someone, communication just happens. This is how it is with the Lord.

Likewise, I can rest content in the presence of God whenever it seems He is "not speaking." Our communication goes deeper than words.

As a new creation in Christ, you "have put on the new man, which is renewed in knowledge after the image of Him that created him."[404] And one of the things the Spirit continually brings us is "knowledge of His will in all wisdom and spiritual understanding."[405] Again, we see interconnectedness between different sevenfold functions: *knowledge, wisdom and understanding.*

Supernatural knowledge is a powerful tool. We know that King Solomon asked God for wisdom, but did you know he also asked for knowledge in the same prayer?

> *"Give me wisdom* ***and knowledge****, that I may lead this people, for who is able to govern this great people of yours?"*

---

[404] Col. 3:10, KJV

[405] Col. 1:9, KJV

> *God said to Solomon, "Since this is your heart's desire and you have not asked for wealth, riches or honor, nor for the death of your enemies, and since you have not asked for a long life but for wisdom and* ***knowledge*** *to govern my people over whom I have made you king, therefore wisdom and knowledge will be given you. And I will also give you wealth, riches and honor, such as no king who was before you ever had and none after you will have."*[406]

I want to emphasize again that it is our loving knowledge of God that counts. And because of this, the mind should be blessed as well. A knowledgeable mind brings untold benefits to one's standard of living. Wealth, riches and honor are fringe benefits – just look at any quality of life statistics comparing college grads to unlearned men. Christianity, throughout the ages, has birthed the greatest minds in academia, civilized societies and been a true source of enlightenment.

A basic impact of the fall of mankind was the loss of intimacy with the Lord. This resulted in a lack of revelation. The world chases learning, as if by it, they can regain access to the keys of life. But we must go to the source. As a believer, we have been restored to His abiding love.

> *And this is my prayer: that your love may abound more and more in knowledge and depth of insight.*[407]

---

[406] 2 Chron. 1:10-12, NIV

[407] Phil. 1:9, NIV

We are now passively growing in this love, but understand that you already fully possess love as a believer. How is this so? Because *God is Love.*

> *... If we love one another,* ***God abides in us****, and* ***His love has been perfected in us.*** *By this we know that we abide in Him, and He in us, because He has given us of His Spirit. ... And we have known and believed the love that God has for us.* ***God is love, and he who abides in love abides in God, and God in him.***[408]

The apostles also write much on how true love spends itself in good deeds, obedience and service to others. We can't say we possess love, and yet disobey God or dislike fellow people. Love is an irresistible force that has to pour itself out like an unrelenting force in your bones. Love is not a work, but you can't help but to care for people when you really are a lover. Speaking of Josiah, the Lord says, "He defended the cause of the poor and needy, and so all went well. Is that not what it means to **know me**?"[409]

The Spirit of Knowledge, by nature, is about the business of loving God and loving others as ourselves.

+ The Spirit of the Fear of the Lord

Now we move on to the seventh and final flow of the Spirit – it is the *Fear of the Lord.* This is perhaps one of the trickiest operations of Holy Spirit to explain, because of our stark misconceptions about the nature of

---

[408] 1 John 4:12-13, 16, NKJV

[409] Jer. 22:16, NIV

God. The *Spirit of the Fear of the Lord* does not sound like a lot of fun to the one who views God as a hard task master. Anyone who has been burned by religious oppression, fear of punishment or joyless Christianity will likely have some erroneous beliefs about this particular operation of the Spirit. Let me start with this beautiful verse:

> *There is no fear in love. But perfect love drives out fear, because fear has to do with punishment. The one who fears is not made perfect in love.*[410]

We see right away why the Spirit of the Fear of the Lord must be intrinsically paired with the Spirit of Intimate Knowledge. Without a deep grasp of God's love, you will always compare this celestial awe to the brutish primal tyranny of earthly fear.

Even a number of secular dictionaries define the fear of the Lord differently than ordinary fear. In fact, the Microsoft Word program dictionary I am using to write this chapter right now places the "fear of the Lord" under the heading of *reverence*, which is "respect or awe for somebody or something." A clear distinction is made from worry, anxiety, horror, panic or an unpleasant feeling caused by the anticipation of danger.

Jesus is the Prince of Peace. He tells us that worry is a sin. Anxiety is a fruit of the old man. Now you bear the fruit of peace.

---

[410] 1 John 4:18, NIV

CHAPTER SIX

+ Delighting in The Fear of the Lord

The fear of the Lord is the only kind of fear that you can *delight* in. This is the only type of truly *pleasurable* or *comforting* fear. The scriptures say that Jesus would *"delight in the fear of the Lord."*[411]

This is the only type of fear that can intoxicate you. We don't normally associate "fear" with "delight." But in fact, the only reason we really fear God is because He is infinitely glad, infinitely beautiful and infinitely good. Imagine Him to be like a billion volts of electric beauty, trying to run through your little two-volt fuse! It blows your circuit board. It's overwhelming. He's so immensely good that it frightens us and we don't have language or context for it.

Not only do we enjoy the fear of God, but this word "delight" literally means to "shine forth" and to "inhale as a fragrance." You glow with the fear of God as it radiates out of you, as a fragrant authority..

We see this pairing of fear and delight – two seemingly contradictory notions – in one of God's names. In Genesis 31, the Lord is named the "Fear of Isaac." And what does *Isaac* mean? Laughter! Isaac is also is a prophetic sign of the promise. God is so happy and His plans are so good for you that it leaves you terrified with joy!

> *All you who fear God, how blessed you are!* ***How happily you walk*** *on His smooth straight road!*[412]

---

[411] Isa. 11:3, NIV

[412] Ps. 128:1, MSG

KNOWLEDGE AND THE FEAR OF THE LORD

Happy is the man that feareth always. ...[413]

When we "understand" the fear the Lord,[414] we actually *want* to tremble in His presence. This is no irrational panic attack. Even His righteous judgments are sent to drive away every hindrance to intimacy and joy. You are not an object of His wrath, because the fullness of that wrath was meted out on His own Son.

+ HE BORE OUR CHASTISEMENT

For a believer, this fear is never in relation to a fear of punishment. Of course, we should always be mindful that stupid actions have bad consequences. Sin still has ramification to our earthly lives. God may truly give His children discipline, but discipline and punishment are different things. Discipline relates to instruction, training and to guiding their paths to direct them toward joyful, fulfilling lives. I may discipline myself to play guitar or write a book. I am not *punishing* myself. We are not objects of His wrath.

Some of the misunderstanding about punishment stems from a misquote of scripture in Hebrews 12. The writer of Hebrews endeavors to quote Proverbs 3:12 when he says:

> *... because the Lord disciplines those He loves, and He punishes everyone He accepts as a son.*[415]

The writer plainly tells us he is quoting scripture, but

---

[413] Prov. 28:14

[414] See Prov. 2:5

[415] Heb. 12:6, NIV

when we look up the actual Old Testament verse he is quoting, the word "punishment" is not there:

> *... because the Lord disciplines those He loves, as a father the son He delights in.*[416]

Regardless of whether this is a scribal error or an inspired addition, you can be sure of this – the punishment of God fell upon *the Son He delights in.* That Son is Jesus. He was chastised for your transgression. Most of this talk you hear about "God brought me out to the woodshed" is hokey pokey bad theology. If God pulled out His belt or wooden spoon to give you a spanking, you would be annihilated in an instant. You couldn't handle the cup of His wrath – one single drop of which would drag you down to the uttermost recesses of hell.

+ The Beginning of Wisdom

I don't mean to water down the fear of the Lord by defining it *only* as "reverent awe" or "respect." It is not an oppressive fear, but nevertheless it can be a *real* terror!

This fear should manifest differently for the nonbeliever and the saint. For the nonbeliever, it is indeed a fear of punishment. The fear of hell and the prospects of damnation should be as real as breathing and as horrible as his twisted imagination will allow.

Let the sinner smell the sulphur and brimstone. Let him hear the hounds of hell, the gnashing of teeth and consider the prospect of eternal separation from God. But let it drive him home to the loving arms of a saviour.

---

416 Prov. 3:12, NIV

Although I don't agree with his approach, there is some truth in what John Wesley said. He instructed his pastors to teach ninety percent law and only ten percent grace. His reasoning was that people would get so frustrated by their inability to follow the law they would eventually give up and turn to Jesus.

Jesus Himself was not a grace preacher. He preached law to its utmost extent. The point of His teaching and parables was to *frustrate* us. To show how powerless we are to uphold the law on our own, and to chase us into the arms of a savior. In His earthly ministry, Jesus was the last Old Covenant preacher. He *did* talk of grace, but only preached it fully through His triumphant act on the cross. After that, the era of grace unfolded, which He began to preach through the apostle Paul. The New Covenant had begun.

The scriptures tell us that, "The law of the Lord is perfect, converting the soul. ..."[417] Now we know that the law doesn't save us. Faith does. What this verse means is that the law was made to *convict* sinners. And the kindness of God then enters to lead us to repentance. The law doesn't save us, but it served as a school master, pointing us to the Lord.

For the independent sinner, who refuses to trust Jesus, the *fear of the Lord is the beginning of wisdom.* In the days of Wesley and Whitefield, tens of thousands of people would be moaning in fear and agony, even beating themselves, as the revivalists preached on repentance. Some would even go away from the meetings

---

[417] Ps. 19:7, KJV

with nosebleeds and their physical bones out of joint, because of their fitful agonizing over sin.

Today, people think that this is what true revival should look like – lots of people beating themselves up and getting depressed. However, Wesley and Whitefield know that this agony over sin did not reflect *true conversion.* Whitefield himself spoke of the tens of thousands who became fearful – but only the few who moved on to *unspeakable joy* were the ones he considered to be truly saved.[418]

Christianity is not marked by self-defeatism. It is marked by happy trust in a savior.

John the Beloved, the love disciple, snuggled on Jesus' breast in the synoptic gospels. But when He sees the Lord in a different dimension – as the Lord of Glory in Revelation 1, John hits the dirt! He falls on the ground as though he were dead. You would probably do the same thing. He is the Lord of Hosts, the King of the armies of Heaven. An all-consuming fire.

However, you must notice as soon as John fell down, Jesus put His right hand on him and said, "Do not be afraid."[419] Whenever a man in scripture encountered the Lord or an angel in manifest form, they consistently had to be told, "Do not fear!"

We must come boldly before His throne. We are not to have a slavish fear like a dog when we approach Him.

---

418 For a more extensive look at Whitefield and Wesley, see my earlier book, *The Ecstasy of Loving God* (Shippensburg, PA: Destiny Image Publishers, 2009).

419 See Rev. 1:17

He is our Father. And any other emotion besides pure joy and delight is a declaration that His nature is somehow less good than it really is. Never mistake joy and happiness as being irreverent, rude, rebellious or blasphemous toward Him.

+ The Myth of Reverence

So if the believer has no fear of eternal punishment, then how does the fear of the Lord relate to him? Well, it is still not merely a "reverence" per se. Let me explain.

To merely say that the fear of God is simply *reverence*, somehow takes away its punch. The common notion of *reverence* is often a conjured, bland uncomfortable type of corporate melancholy that you find in stuffy old churches. It is reminiscent of a funeral dirge. This is not true reverence, nor is it the fear of the Lord.

The fear of the Lord is sill a very *real* fear. But let's think in terms of *adventure* rather than punishment. Mankind is built to fear. We all have a normal, healthy capacity to fear something – and that desire has to be satisfied. Why do you think people are drawn to horror movies, extreme sports, bungee jumping, roller coasters and the like?

Everyone has a healthy craving for the *unknown* ... for the uncontrollable. There's something gloriously terrifying about knowing that God is real, and that He can do whatever He wants to do! We want real fear without the oppression.

+ An Anointing of Fear

Now that we've explained the basis of holy fear a bit, let's remember that the Spirit of the Fear of the Lord is *personified.* This is much more than an individual's personal "sense" of fear. It is one of the sevenfold *anointings* that rests on you. In other words, the fear of the Lord is not just something you do – be afraid of Him – it is actually a *person* that emanates from you. Jesus is the Fear of the Lord. When you are anointed with the fear of the Lord, this does not mean that you are simply walking around, trembling with terror. Instead, you are carrying an atmosphere or a *metron* of Glory around you. As you are walking down the street, anyone who comes into your radius begins to experience the authority or even the terror of God. It is a tangible, transferrable anointing that possesses you. Demand for His reverence exudes from you to everyone around you – even if you are unaware of it.

Smith Wigglesworth once walked into a grocery store. He didn't say a word, but three people fell to the floor, repenting of their sins. We have all heard the stories of how he would meet a complete stranger or a passerby, who exclaimed, "Sir, you convict me of sin!" Sometimes, he would simply say "hello" to someone in passing and they would scream and cry out to the Lord![420]

Charles Finney is another person who seemed to particularly manifest this anointing. Even Finney's face looks scary in old photographs! One day in upper New York, prior to one of his meetings, he decided to take an afternoon stroll through a nearby textile factory. He

---

420 John Crowder, *The New Mystics*, 307-308.

had not preached a word, nor announced his name to anyone. As he was walking silently along, his very presence began to make people shake with terror. He noticed two particular women who looked very agitated at his being there.

> *I went slowly toward them. They saw me coming and were evidently much excited. One of them was trying to mend a broken thread, but I observed that her hands trembled so that she could not mend it. I approached slowly, looking on each side at the machinery as I passed, but observed that this girl grew more and more agitated and could not proceed with her work. When I came within eight or ten feet of her I looked solemnly at her. She observed it and was quite overcome, and sank down and burst into tears. The impression caught like powder, and in a few moments nearly all in the room were in tears.*
>
> *This feeling spread throughout the factory. The owner of the establishment was present and seeing the state of things he said to the superintendent, "Stop the mill and let the people attend to religion, for it is more important that our souls should be saved than that this factory run."*[421]

The revival swept the factory for days, as people from the rafters to the cellar packed the place for days of preaching – almost every single factory worker was saved. This is similar to what happened in the early days of the Pensacola/Brownsville revival in the early

---

[421] Charles Finney, *The Autobiography of Charles G. Finney* (Minneapolis, MN: Bethany House Publishers, 1977), 124-125.

1990s. Thousands would run to the altar, as a tangible sense of God's dread swept over them.

I have had massive, brawny men run away from me in fear, just because I offered to pray for them. Once, we were on the streets in Britain, when an outbreak of Glory started knocking people over and folks began to get saved in the marketplace. Thousands of people were walking by witnessing it all happen, and so police came up to see what was going on. My friend offered to pray for the police officer, and the cop was filled with dread! The officer ran away in the fear of the Lord. My friend turned and chased the police down the street to pray for them! It looked like a backwards police chase.

+ Scaring Dirty Cops

There is a tangible sense of authority on you when the Spirit of the Fear of the Lord manifests in your life. We once took a team of about thirty people to Indonesia to minister to the poor. While we were there, we took a couple days to vacation and rented some moped scooters to cruise around for sightseeing.

One particular day, we were driving when some police pulled us over. They took our registration papers and began threatening to take us into the station. Like many police in developing nations, these were dirty cops using their authority to get a bribe from us. They asked us how much money we had, and were bent on taking every last penny from us.

"We're not giving you any money," we said. "If you want a bribe, you had better come with us!"

Of course, these men had the natural authority to haul us in and drag us into a sleazy little jail cell. Yet there was authority *on us*, not *them*. We physically snatched the registration papers right back out of the cops' hands, confidently got back on our scooters and drove away. The police just stood there, with fear evident in their shifty eyes!

They were scared to do anything to us. Yet their greed couldn't be stopped. They drove along and grabbed another unsuspecting member of our team, likewise pulling him over to the shoulder of the road. Just as this person was about to pay them a bribe, we saw what was happening. We pulled our bikes over again, and said, "Don't give them any money!"

The cops froze again, frustrated! Somehow they knew they were powerless against us. As we drove away, they stood there angry, yet fearful – one of them said in his broken English, "You suck!"

+ "We Perceive You are a Prophet"

Another time this tangible authority manifested was in India, when I was hosting a massive evangelism crusade. We had planned this huge event for months, spending tens of thousands of dollars in preparations. The first night's meeting had finally arrived. The swarming crowds were gathered – everything was in place – and I was about to go up and preach to the people. Suddenly, the local officials, influenced by Hindu radicals, issued a governmental order for me not to minister. As I sat there, an official document was placed in my hand, stating that I did not have a religious visa.

There was even a politician in attendance, his guard armed with machine guns.

I could feel the fire of God on me. I knew that souls were about to be saved. I didn't care if I landed in jail – I would preach the gospel.

The crusade organizers begged me to be patient. They asked me not to preach that night, and to just give them another day to sort it out with the officials.

"Wait until tomorrow to preach," they said. "But tonight, only introduce yourself to the people."

When I picked up the microphone, the thick, tangible presence of God became so weighty; I could feel the entire atmosphere change. It took only a second for the power of God to smack the place, and yet I was only introducing myself. In just a moment, my coordinator dashed up to me.

"Go ahead! Preach! Preach!" he said. "The officials have *perceived* that you are a prophet!"

Of course I hate silly charismatic titles and would never have *called myself* a prophet. But there was such a powerful anointing that the Lord Himself validated me.

The atmosphere that was present struck conviction into unbelieving hearts of the officials, and it brought favor. Over the course of the next few days, we saw countless miracles and more than 100,000 decisions for Christ.

+ Dread Champions

In the coming days, Christians are no longer going to be the subject of mockery and derision as they are now. Be assured that in these last days, we were told that scoffers would come. But their scoffing will find a swift end as the sons of God manifest the full weight of His power and Glory.

The prophet Joel speaks of the dread this triumphant church strikes into the heart of darkness. These are the fearsome ones who will drip with a tangible atmosphere of the Spirit of the Fear of the Lord:

> *With a noise like that of chariots they leap over the mountaintops, like a crackling fire consuming stubble, like a mighty army drawn up for battle. At the sight of them, nations are in anguish; every face turns pale. They charge like warriors; they scale walls like soldiers. They all march in line, not swerving from their course. They do not jostle each other; each marches straight ahead. They plunge through defenses without breaking ranks. They rush upon the city; they run along the wall. They climb into the houses; like thieves they enter through the windows. Before them the Earth shakes, the sky trembles, the sun and moon are darkened, and the stars no longer shine. The Lord thunders at the head of His army; His forces are beyond number, and mighty are those who obey His command. The day of the Lord is great; it is dreadful. Who can endure it?*[422]

---

[422] Joel 2:5-11, NIV

Christianity will no longer be spoken of as a byword. Just as in the early days of the church, great awe will fill the people and we will be deemed in high respect by the nations.

+ No More Fear of Man

The fear of the Lord is either a thing of beautiful splendor or utter horror, depending on which side of the cross you are on!

Most people only know the slavish fear of man, and have never been liberated by the delight of the fear of the Lord. In Jeremiah 1:17, the Lord tells the prophet to essentially "terrify or be terrified." That's our choice! Your circumstances will frighten you, or else you will operate in an authority that terrifies your adversaries.

It is impossible to have the fear of God and the fear of man abiding in the same vessel. Proverbs 29:25 says, "The fear of man brings a snare." Furthermore, we should know that the fear of man is one of the primary roots of religion. Jesus told the Pharisees, "You are those who justify yourselves in the sight of men, but God knows your hearts; for that which is highly esteemed among men is detestable in the sight of God."[423]

Rick Joyner writes, "If we truly fear the Lord, we will not fear anyone else. To honor and respect the Lord is to be delivered from all fear of man."[424] And also the

---

[423] Luke 16:15, NASB

[424] Joyner, *There Were Two Trees in the Garden*, 123.

apostle Paul states, "If I were still trying to please men, I would not be a bond-servant of Christ."[425]

If you do not fear God – in the proper context of the word – you are already in bondage to the fear of man. *Man pleasing* is ultimately a form of cowardice, and is on the top list of qualifications for being tossed into the lake of fire![426] Doesn't that seem a paradoxical statement? *Don't be afraid or you'll go to hell!* Doesn't the very concept of hell strike cowardly fear? No! Not if you're a believer. You are no longer a coward, but the Valliant Warrior lives inside of you.

"Our ministry will be false to the degree that it is affected by the fear of man," adds Joyner.[427] He notes that we are to be servants of all, but man is never to become our master. Even your service and honor toward men should be a form of worship to God. As Paul states, "With good will render service, as to the Lord, and not to men."[428]

Being a Christian is all about your oppressive fear of man melting into a true wonderment over God. David said, "Let me fall into the hands of the Lord, for His mercy is very great; but do not let me fall into the hands of men."[429]

---

[425] Gal. 1:10, NASB

[426] See Rev. 21:8

[427] Rick Joyner, *There Were Two Trees in the Garden*, 124.

[428] Eph. 6:7, NASB

[429] 2 Sam. 24; 1 Chron. 21, NIV

CHAPTER SIX

+ Rewards of Divine Fear

As with the Spirit of Wisdom, the Bible lists a specific number of benefits to those who walk in the Spirit of the Fear of the Lord. These include happiness, a rewarding spouse, prosperity, protection from loss, long life, anointed children and many other general blessings. A concise list of these incentives are found in Psalm 128:

> *Blessed* (happy, fortunate, to be envied) *are all who fear the Lord, who walk in His ways. You will eat the fruit of your labor; blessings and prosperity will be yours. Your wife will be like a fruitful vine within your house; your sons will be like olive shoots around your table. Thus is the man blessed who fears the Lord. May the Lord bless you from Zion all the days of your life; may you see the prosperity of Jerusalem, and may you live to see your children's children. Peace be upon Israel.*[430]

The Proverbs furthermore tell us that the fear of the Lord is a fountain of life; it turns us from the snares of death; it gives us and our children a place of refuge; it causes us to abide in satisfaction; and it keeps us from being visited with evil.

The fear of the Lord is also connected to receiving revelation, for He "confides in those who fear Him."[431] And would you like an angelic visitation? The angel of the Lord also encamps around those who fear Him, and He

---

430 Ps. 128, NIV notes mine

431 Ps. 25:14, NIV

delivers them.[432] And how about this – *"those who fear Him lack nothing."*[433]

> *The fear of the Lord adds length of life, but the years of the wicked are cut short.*[434]

> *Humility and the fear of the Lord bring wealth and honor and life.*[435]

+ A Double Cord

Another great way to simply define the fear of the Lord is to *love God and hate evil.*

If you only have a fear of punishment, but no love of God, it will eventually propel you to run from Him. The power of the law is its fear of punishment. The power of grace is its unconditional love. It's not just man pleasing that we need to be liberated from, but also *God pleasing!* Your efforts don't appease the Lord one iota.

> *Convinced that no human being can please God by self-improvement, we believed in Jesus as Messiah so that we might be set right before God by trusting in the Messiah, not by trying to be good.*[436]

Without a revelation of grace, you will misunderstand the fear of the Lord. Again, we see how the double cord of proper *fear* and intimate *knowledge* must intrinsi-

---

432 See Ps. 34:7

433 Ps. 34:9, NIV

434 Prov. 10:27, NIV

435 Prov. 22:4, NIV

436 Gal. 2:16, MSG

cally work together. The Book of Proverbs says, "The fear of the Lord is the beginning of knowledge. ..."[437]

Let us grow up from slavish notions of punishment and become secure in our sonship. We never abandon the fear of the Lord, but we begin to rightly understand it. We must grow into a maturity that manifests the perfect *love* of God. Fear of punishment will produce an immediate response, but only the love of God will produce a sustained, happy relationship. The fear of God may rightly challenge us to live righteous, pure lives – but this fear is never divorced from love. It's swallowed up by it. Love becomes the reason. Righteous living cannot take hold in the depths of our heart without us being enraptured by the goodness and beauty of the Lord.

To fear God is not masochistic. It is actually to choose life and liberty and blessing. Romans 8 says:

> *...because those who are led by the Spirit of God are sons of God. For you did not receive a spirit that makes you a slave again to fear, but you received the Spirit of sonship. And by Him we cry, "Abba, Father." The Spirit Himself testifies with our spirit that we are God's children.*[438]

The fear of the Lord is the beginning of wisdom. The love of God is highest wisdom.

---

437 Prov. 1:7, NIV

438 Rom. 8: 14-16, NIV

+ Chapter Seven
The Sons of Golden Oil

What a privilege to live in these days of God's presence and power, as the church is finally discovering the untold riches of her inheritance in Christ. There is such a need in the Earth today for the church to fully demonstrate the heart, mind, Glory and power of God. As a people discover they are completely full in Christ – lacking nothing – the word of Christ's finished work will birth faith. And that faith – trusting in the reality of our union – will produce *substance.*

We know that all things are possible for those that believe. And again we are called to do *greater things* than even the miracles wrought by Christ.[439] For it is still Christ who is working and willing to do His good pleasure through us – the church – who are His very hands and feet in the Earth.

There have been untold predictions of a coming generation who would operate in the full manifestation of their sonship. All of creation – the very elements of the Earth – long for the children of God to shine forth their true identity. Polluted rivers in the poorest places of the Earth will be turned to sweet water. Deserts in North Africa will blossom into tropical gardens. Signs in the heavens and on the Earth below. Political tyrants will crumble into a pool of repentant tears at the word of the Lord. Nations will see revivals erupt like a chemical reaction and sweep through their entire populace in a single day. Certain ministers will be particularly known for regrowing missing limbs,

---

[439] See John 14:12

while others will clear out morgues with the ease of faith.

These are but trivial matters. The real source and rally cry of it all will be a return to the simple, childlike reality of effortless union with God.

Because of Christ's work, all who trust in Him are sons. And sonship is not something we are climbing or working our way into. The manifestation of sonship is as simple as believing Christ's cross was enough to seal your adoption into the family. Unlike times past, we will not be lured from the promise by trying to labor for family status. Nor can we make ourselves be who we are. We are sons.

We are sons who are dripping with the oil of bliss. We are the candlesticks flowing with the full measure of this sevenfold torrent of golden oil.

The prophet Zechariah wondered at the two olive trees and the lampstand which he saw in the vision. When Zechariah asked the angel to interpret the meaning of the two olive trees and the candlestick, the angel replied with a word to the governor Zerubbabel saying, "not by might, nor by power but by my Spirit." So the answer to Zechariah's question as to the olive trees and their meanings were that they were *anointings* of the Spirit of God: *by my Spirit.*[440]

Further on, the Lord brings clarity to this question, as Zechariah repeats his question:

---

[440] See Zech. 4:6

Again I asked him, "What are these two olive branches beside the two gold pipes that pour out golden oil?"
He replied, "Do you not know what these are?"
"No, my lord," I said.
So he said, "These are the two who are anointed to serve the Lord of all the Earth."[441]

We see these two anointed ones mentioned again in the Book of Revelation – the two end time witnesses who prophesy in sackcloth for 1,260 days.

These are the two olive trees and the two lampstands which stand before the Lord of the Earth.[442]

Of course the identity of the two olive trees – the two witnesses – is a subject of great wonder. But without any guesswork, we can glean much from what the scriptures do plainly tell us. For starters, John sees that they are endowed with great power.

And if anyone wants to harm them, fire proceeds from their mouth and devours their enemies. And if anyone wants to harm them, he must be killed in this manner. These have power to shut heaven, so that no rain falls in the days of their prophecy; and they have power over waters to turn them to blood, and to strike the Earth with all plagues, as often as they desire.[443]

---

[441] Zech. 4:12-14, NIV
[442] Rev. 11:4, RSV
[443] Rev. 11:5-6, NKJV

These sons of oil have infinite power flowing through their pipes. The olive tree – the source of the anointing oil – is directly feeding them. The addition of the bowl to the candlestick is Christ Himself. He is the reservoir and channel to our ceaseless supply of oil. This oil causes us to burn a perpetual light. God's full sevenfold river flows continually through us.

+ MOSES AND ELIJAH

In reading the passage above, we see that the two witnesses operate in the same miraculous powers as Moses and Elijah. Moses turned waters to blood and struck the Earth with plagues. Elijah shut up the heavens and called down fire.

Are these two literal people? And are they literally Moses and Elijah? Time will tell. But let us not be too primitive in our understanding. Let's see the bigger picture. It's not about two people; it's about the Lord. These represent a two-fold *anointing* that will cover the entire church. We are going to walk in the fullness of what both Moses and Elijah represented.

I believe that Moses and Elijah represented the law and the prophets. But furthermore, they are symbolic of the Word and the Spirit.

> *Yet a time is coming and has now come when the true worshipers will worship the Father in spirit and truth, for they are the kind of worshipers the Father seeks. God is spirit, and His worshipers must worship in spirit and in truth.*[444]

---

[444] John 4:23-24, NIV

The Word of God and Spirit of God are inseparable. Holy Spirit is the *Spirit of Truth* who always reflects Jesus, the Living Word.

> *When the Counselor comes, whom I will send to you from the Father, the Spirit of Truth who goes out from the Father, He will testify about me.*[445]

Moses received the Torah – the *law* of God. Elijah, on the other hand, represented the prophetic in its most mystical dimension. Like the fleeting wind or a flowing river, Elijah's movements could not be pinned down or anticipated. He was an ecstatic prophet and his movements defied human comprehension.[446] Elijah was not a psalmist or a writing prophet, but rather his life was an *embodiment* of his message. He was a signs prophet, and represented God's *Spirit*.

On the Mount of Transfiguration in Luke 9, we see that Jesus met with Moses and Elijah. Peter, in his inept understanding of the situation, offered to build them all tents. Silly Peter! The scriptures tell us, "He did not know what he was saying."[447] The Father basically said, "Shush ... Listen to Jesus." They did not need tents, because a cloud of Glory came and enveloped them. They came from the cloud and they abide in that cloud.

We shouldn't think of the two witnesses in a strictly naturalistic sense. Nevertheless, Moses and Elijah

---

[445] John 15:26, NIV

[446] See 1 Kings 18:12

[447] Luke 9:33, NIV

must have appeared quite physical for Peter to suggest building an earthly accommodation for them. Elijah's body was physically whisked away to Heaven. He never died. There's no reason God couldn't send Him back.

Moses, on the other hand, did die. But remember that he represents the word – a foreshadow of the Incarnate Word. Jesus said the word is a seed, and what must the seed do to bear fruit? It must first *die.*[448] Is it possible that Moses was or is to be resurrected? We do know that the archangel Michael wrestled with the devil for the body of Moses.[449] There must have been a reason for this.

Both Moses and Elijah are men who *transferred* the anointing they carried onto their protégés. Elijah gave it to Elisha, while Moses laid hands on Joshua. Also, we are familiar with the prophet Malachi's statement about sending the sending Elijah before great day of the Lord. But did you ever notice the verse just prior to that?

> *Remember the law of my servant* ***Moses****, the decrees and laws I gave him at Horeb for all Israel. See, I will send you the prophet* ***Elijah*** *before that great and dreadful day of the Lord comes.*[450]

Notice that Moses and Elijah are paired together again. Jesus said that John the Baptist was the Elijah to come. He prepared the way for the coming of

---

[448] See John 12:24
[449] See Jude 9
[450] Mal. 4:4-5, NIV

Christ. But I believe an entire generation will be clothed in this prophetic Elijah spirit before the second coming of Christ. The so-called "spirit of Elijah" is nothing less than a term to describe Holy Spirit Himself – in the way we would call Him the *God of Abraham, Isaac and Jacob.*

To say Moses is returning, or that we should "remember his law" does not mean a reversal back to legalism or the jot and tittle of the Old Covenant. Be clear about this. Christ is the fulfillment of the law, and that fulfillment is *love*. We have a *better word* and participate in a covenant that is so bright it eclipses the Glory of the former one. Now, when we remember the law, we should remember Christ, it's fulfillment.

Interestingly, the first Pentecost – *Shavuot* – happened with Moses as He received the Torah on Mt. Sinai. There, the law was given. But on the fulfillment of Pentecost, in Acts 2, Holy Spirit was given. Moses had the law written on tablets of stone, but in Acts 2, the law was written on human hearts. Remember that Pentecost is the fiftieth day following the seven weeks. For Moses, Pentecost happened fifty days after crossing the Red Sea. For the apostles, Pentecost happened fifty days after the resurrection of Christ.

When the law was given to Moses, three thousand died in their sins. When Holy Spirit was poured out in Acts 2, three thousand came to salvation and eternal life. Pentecost is the feast of first fruits, or *harvest*.

We are a generation that is living in the greatest era of harvest the Earth has ever known. You have power to bear fruit, much fruit and fruit that will remain. There is a harvest Glory that will make evangelism easy and bountiful. As you read this book, understand that you are closer to the end times than any man that has ever walked the Earth. You are living in a tremendous era. The ancients longed to look into your day – an era when men would be in perfect union with God. Deepest communion – untold revelation and power – they are all at your disposal as a temple flowing with fullness. Maybe you've been throwing your net over the boat for a long day's night. But in one fell swoop, your nets are going to be full because it's not your efforts that count – it's Christ's commissioning. Know that harvest is not an owed duty. It's your rightful inheritance.

These two witnesses are like the two loaves that were offered on Pentecost – the only loaves ever offered with leaven in them – this twofold sacrifice represented your old sinful nature dying *together* with Christ. And now you are a new creation flowing with perpetual love and power.

+ JOSHUA AND ZERUBBABEL

We can't be too adamantly literalistic on our predictions of two future individual witnesses. Again, the greatest implication is that we are *all* sons of oil, operating in a twofold mantle of everything these two trees represent.

If you want to get absolutely specific, the Bible tells us verbatim who these two men are. Contextually,

Zechariah is talking about two men – Joshua the high priest and Zerubbabel, the prince of Judah. These two were *symbolic of things to come.*

> *These are the two sons of oil [Joshua the high priest and Zerubbabel the prince of Judah] – the two anointed ones – who stand before the Lord of the whole Earth [as His anointed instruments].*[451]

Zerubbabel was a civil ruler who, together with the priest Joshua, was leading the Israelites back from their long Babylonian captivity. He was in charge of rebuilding the temple of the Lord.

Both of these men represent Christ – our High Priest and builder of His church. Likewise, they represent two mantles on us as believers. One is a king. Another is a priest.

> *But you are a chosen people, a **royal priesthood**, a holy nation, a people belonging to God, that you may declare the praises of Him who called you out of darkness into His wonderful light.*[452]

We will explore the meaning of this "royal priesthood" in just a moment. Understand that Zerubbabel and Joshua were the primary figures in Zechariah's prophecy. Zechariah received his vision the night before he was to ordain Joshua to the priesthood. Not to be confused with the Joshua of Moses' day, this high priest *Yeshua* was symbolic of the true Messiah to come, our eternal High Priest.

---

[451] Zech. 4:14, AMP

[452] 1 Pet. 2:9, NIV

+ The High Priest

Zechariah saw Joshua in filthy clothes, which represented the sin of humanity borne upon Christ. The Lord rebuked satan and stripped away the filthiness from Joshua. The Lord said, "See, I have removed your iniquity from you, and I will clothe you with rich robes."[453]

> *"Listen, O high priest Joshua and your associates seated before you, who are men* ***symbolic of things to come****: I am going to bring my servant,* ***the Branch****. See, the stone I have set in front of Joshua! There are* ***seven eyes on that one stone****, and I will engrave an inscription on it," says the Lord Almighty, "and* ***I will remove the sin of this land in a single day****."*[454]

The role of the high priest is to make atonement for the sin of the people. Christ alone could do this. Christ alone could suffer. Christ alone could redeem. Woe to that intercessor who thinks she assists Christ in bearing the burdens of the world! There is no assistance to His cross. On the road of His passion, He said, "weep not for me."[455] You are not even to feel sorry for His sufferings. You are called to rejoice and feast on them. Commentator Adam Clarke writes:

> *Many pious persons have been greatly distressed in their minds, because they could not weep on*

---

[453] Zech. 3:4, NKJV

[454] Zech. 3:8-9, NIV

[455] See Luke 23:28

reading or hearing of the sufferings of Christ. For the relief of all such, let it be for ever known that no human spirit can possibly take any part in the passion of the Messiah. His sufferings were such as only God manifested in the flesh could bear; and, as they were all of an expiatory nature, no man can taste of or share in them. Besides, the sufferings of Christ are not a subject of sorrow to any man; but on the contrary, of eternal rejoicing to the whole of a lost world. Some have even prayed to participate in the sufferings of Christ. ... Relative to this point, there are many unwarrantable expressions used by religious people in their prayers and hymns. To give only one instance, how often do we hear these or similar words said or sung, "Give me to feel thy agonies! One drop of thy sad cup afford!" Reader! One drop of this cup would bear down thy soul to endless ruin; and these agonies would annihilate the universe. He suffered alone: for of the people there was none with Him; because His sufferings were to make an atonement for the sins of the world: and in the work of redemption He had no helper.[456]

If we are now ordained as priests, sharing in the priestly office of Christ – what is left for us to accomplish? If the work is finished and done, who are we to hold such a title as priest? Our priesthood duty is found in the verse we read earlier:

But you are a chosen people, a royal priesthood, a holy nation, a people belonging to God, ***that you***

---

[456] Clarke, *Commentary on the Whole Bible*, Excerpt from Luke 23.

> ***may declare the praises of Him*** *who called you out of darkness into His wonderful light.*[457]

Our job is not to repeat what He has done. Rather, it is to simply to rejoice in what He is done! As John Piper says, "God is most glorified in us when we are most satisfied in Him." As a priest, you also *declare* what He has done. Priests minister to God and the people. You minister to Him through the glad worship of your heart. And you now minister to the people as a mouthpiece of the finished realities of union with God. You are a bold declarer of the scandalous grace of the gospel. A New Testament priest worships God and preaches the gospel. He is not a mediator, but rather points to and rejoices in the Mediator:

> *For there is one God and one Mediator between God and men, the Man Christ Jesus.*[458]

+ A King and a Priest

The Branch of Jesse was to be both King and Priest – a double office with a double anointing.

> *It is He who will build the temple of the Lord, and He will be clothed with majesty and will sit and rule on His throne.* ***And He will be a priest on His throne****. And there will be harmony between the two.*[459]

---

[457] 1 Pet. 2:9, NIV

[458] 1 Tim. 2:5, NKJV

[459] Zech. 6:13, NIV

SONS OF GOLDEN OIL

In every worldly society, there is conflict between the two offices of civil and spiritual authority. Government and spirituality never mix well – and church history proves this true. But when Christ sits as King and Priest, "the counsel of peace shall be between them both."[460]

The holy anointing oil Zechariah saw was a twofold anointing of both King and Priest. This represents both earthly authority and heavenly authority.

Another dimension of the two witnesses is this: *they are Heaven and Earth.*

Heaven and Earth both testify to the gospel, as both are reconciled in the gospel. When the kingly and priestly offices are rightly joined, there is harmony between the natural and the supernatural. The unseen word, in a sense, is *incarnate*.

The twofold anointing of both king and priest was prefigured in the life of King David. He wore the linen ephod and ate the shewbread – both were legally set aside only for the priest, not a king. Christ now sits on David's throne.

David was also a prophet. In fact, Christ has a *threefold* office of prophet, priest and king. Remember that the two olive trees are also called two "prophets."[461] In addition, there was another prototype of this threefold office in scripture – *Melchizedek*. He was the king of Salem who offered Abraham the bread and

---

[460] Zech. 6:13, ESV

[461] See Rev. 11:10

wine – a type of Christ – and received a tithe from him. Jesus came in the "order of Melchizedek."

+ The Kingly Office

I personally believe that Zerubbabel is one of the most understated figures in the scriptures. He represents Christ as King, and also the authoritative dimension of the believer in the natural affairs of the Earth. Note that Zerubbabel, though building with natural stones, was still laboring toward a spiritual end – that of building God's temple.

> *So he answered and said to me: "This is the word of the Lord to Zerubbabel: 'Not by might nor by power, but by My Spirit,' says the Lord of hosts. 'Who are you, O great mountain? Before Zerubbabel you shall become a plain! And he shall bring forth the capstone with shouts of "Grace, grace to it!"'" Moreover the word of the Lord came to me, saying: "The hands of Zerubbabel have laid the foundation of this temple; his hands shall also finish it. Then you will know that the Lord of hosts has sent Me to you. For who has despised the day of small things? For these seven rejoice to see the plumb line in the hand of Zerubbabel. They are the eyes of the Lord, which scan to and fro throughout the whole Earth."*[462]

This corresponds to Christ's finishing work – with shouts of *grace, grace*! How would you like for your earthly career or occupation to be so infused with this great grace, that your job feels more like a vacation

---

[462] Zech. 4:6-11, NKJV

than a laborious task? Adam worked in the garden, but he didn't break a sweat. He didn't strive or toil.

Grace and favor can freely flow through worry-free areas of our life. Worry and anxiety are the antithesis of peace. And peace is the atmosphere where God manifests His oil of authority. Melchizedek was the King of Salem – the *King of Peace*.

Mountains can supernaturally level for you and low places rise up to meet your feet on even ground. It is time to return to *garden works* like Adam experienced. Where the supernatural dimensions of grace meet our earthly callings. This realm only opens up through f*aith* – that is, through trust. Trusting that the whole wide world is in His hands! The more we trust God with the natural affairs of our lives, the less likely we are to stress out, micromanage and worry. It sets us up for miraculous breakthroughs. It allows the oil of favor to bring ease and increase.

The Lord wants us to bear more fruit with less personal effort. This comes through a realization of our authority over the natural realm. Moreover, it comes through realizing that we are not called to bear burdens, but that Christ is the burden bearer. He carries the government on His shoulders.

> *For unto us a child is born, unto us a son is given: and the* ***government shall be upon His shoulder****: and His name shall be called Wonderful, Counsellor, The mighty God, The everlasting Father, The Prince of Peace. Of the* ***increase of His government*** *and peace there shall be no end, upon the* ***throne of David****, and upon His Kingdom, to order*

it, and to establish it with judgment and with justice from henceforth even for ever. The zeal of the Lord of hosts will perform this.[463]

While the church teaches much on priesthood, little attention is afforded to the kingly office of the believer. This office relates to our natural, civil affairs of authority in the Earth. It concerns our careers, occupations, callings and vocational destinies in this life. It concerns rulership, monetary affairs and administration of earthly goods. It speaks of natural influence over people groups.

Of course, Christians are taught to work hard, to be diligent with their hands and to be good stewards. But little emphasis is given to *ruling* and *reigning* in this life.

Unfortunately, most Christians have little vision for their time on Earth. They are preoccupied with just squeaking by. Because Christ's Kingdom is a spiritual one, this life is considered to be a write-off for most people. They are just counting the days on the calendar until they get to Heaven and have a mansion.

+ Subjugating the Earth

The Jews, on the other hand, went the opposite extreme. They were expecting the Messiah to set up a civil kingdom, and so they missed Him when He came as a peasant, riding on a humble donkey, establishing a spiritual one. Make no doubt about it. Jesus is clear about the idolatry of wealth, basing impor-

---

[463] Isa. 9:6-7, KJV

tance on material standards and wielding control unjustly through brute force. His Kingdom is not *of* this world, but it is *over* this world.

Jesus clearly demonstrated that the natural elements of this world – the very wind and waves – obeyed Him. But He did not use natural power to implement His government – He used the *weakness* of the cross to establish all reign and authority. He instituted humility over control, meekness over pride and the submission of His servant body to overcome tyranny.

The "kingdoms" of this world that are subjugated to Him in Revelation 11 can actually be translated as *kingdom* singular. Plurality would indicate numerous earthly political units which must one-by-one be given over to Christ's rulership. But the singular word indicates that Christ has regained rule over the entire dominion of the Earth as a solitary unit. That which had once been forfeited to satan is now His.

> *The Earth is the Lords and everything in it, the world, and all who live in it.*[464]

Jesus has no problem with the natural world itself. *For God so loved the world. ...*[465] Rather, it is the *spirit of the world* – the fallenness and corruption – which He came to destroy by taking its curse upon Himself. Friendship with worldliness is enmity towards God. But this is no wicked indictment of either redeemed man or the natural cosmos. With His blood

---

[464] Ps. 24:1, NIV

[465] See John 3:16

He "purchased men for God from every tribe and language and people and nation."[466]

In dying to the world, Christ purchased it. In a similar way, by not idolizing natural things, they find their proper role. Your physical body makes a wonderful servant but a terrible master. The same is true with money. You will either serve money or money will serve you. God never said money was evil – only the *love of it.* When we seek first Him and His Kingdom, all these natural things are added to us. Wealth, fame and power can be horrible masters or wonderful tools.

A righteous king does not reject the tool, but submits it to the Lord.

My point is that Jesus never diminished the importance of natural authority – He even gave to Caesar what was his. It's just that Jesus emphasized the overarching importance of spiritual authority as the bottom line. The world is not the problem. The problem is idolatry of the world. It's an issue of priority of the heart.

Jesus gained the whole world, but His means of accomplishing this and His *modus operandi* were completely opposite of the world system.

+ A Future Kingdom?

Now, Jesus has commissioned us to boldly reign over the Earth by the Spirit and the Word. We have forgotten this important verse:

---

[466] Rev. 5:9, NIV

> *The kingdom of the world has become the Kingdom of our Lord and of His Christ, and He will reign for ever and ever.*[467]

You may ask: *isn't that in the future? After the breaking of the seventh seal?* Every seal is broken in Christ. He is the lamb who is worthy to open every seal. A complete victory was achieved on the cross, and every kingdom has come under His dominion.

> *And there was given Him dominion, and Glory, and a Kingdom, that all people, nations, and languages, should serve Him: His dominion is an everlasting dominion, which shall not pass away, and His Kingdom that which shall not be destroyed.*[468]

One of the greatest misconceptions plaguing Christendom is the concept that Jesus is only a *future* King. Everyone is waiting for a millennial reign where He will somehow establish a coming kingdom over the Earth. By projecting this kingly role to a future dispensation, we fall into a number of problems:

1. We diminish the role of the cross as the champion event that subjugated the Earth under His control and reversed the entire curse of the fall.

2. We neglect our role as *princes who rule in righteousness*. This abdication of our own authority is as disgraceful as Saul hiding among the

---

[467] Rev. 11:15b, NIV

[468] Dan. 7:14, KJV

baggage when he was meant to lead the people into victory.

Jesus is not just a future king. He is the King of Kings and the Lord of Lords right here and now. Kim Riddlebarger makes some great points in his article *The Triple Cure: Jesus Christ – Our Prophet, Priest and King*:

> *The biblical writers would have been quite mystified, I think, at much of the evangelical discussion about "making Christ Lord" – as though it was through a decision on our part that Christ becomes "the Lord over our lives." And they certainly would have been perplexed by those who insist on reading the kingdom language of the New Testament through the grid of the American nationalism of the Christian right, or the moralistic social gospel of the Christian left. They would, I think, be equally confused by our dispensational brethren, who insist on undercutting the present reign of Christ by arguing that Christ's kingly office (especially the regnum gratiae – the "kingdom of grace") does not come fully into view until a future millennial age commences and at long last Christ supposedly begins to exercise His full authority from the earthly city of Jerusalem. Most of this confusion comes from a failure to understand this third office of Christ, His kingly rule.*[469]

Scriptures are clear that that "the Lord has established His throne in Heaven, and His Kingdom rules over

---

[469] Kim Riddlebarger, "The Triple Cure: Jesus Christ – Our Prophet, Priest and King" (1995). http://www.graceonlinelibrary.org/articles (accessed July 2010).

all."[470] If God is not king *now*, then who is? Some try to excuse problems in the world by pointing to the delegated authority of the Earth to mankind: *The highest heavens belong to the Lord, but the Earth He has given to man.*[471]

It's true that God delegates, and that our sins were the root of problems here – not Him. But that does not mean that our authority is *separate* from His. In fact, that was the whole problem to begin with. Our concept of a separate existence from God – *or a separate free will* – is the reason our union was broken in the fall. Everyone has a will, but it is not truly *free* outside of *His will*. God is still sovereign, and the only freedom is found in our union with Christ that brought us back into alignment with His glorious reign.

Yes, He is king right now.

> *And what is the exceeding greatness of His power toward us who believe, according to the working of His mighty power which He worked in Christ when He raised Him from the dead and seated Him at His right hand in the heavenly places, far above all principality and power and might and dominion, and every name that is named, not only in this age but also in that which is to come. And He put all things under His feet, and gave Him to be head over all things to the church, which is His body, the fullness of Him who fills all in all.*[472]

---

[470] Ps 103:19, NIV
[471] Ps. 115:16, NIV
[472] Eph. 1:19-23, NKJV

On our own, we were unable to rule the sphere of Earth. Our one attempt in the Garden of Eden to make a decision outside of His government caused the whole thing to get botched. In the same way, only He was able to restore it all on the cross.

Even before the era of the fall, God had already previously laid His plans for reconciliation. Prior to the rebellion, the lamb had been slain from the foundation of the Earth to quench it. Never has a moment passed by where God was not on the throne. Now that Christ has been manifest, He says, "All things have been delivered to me by my Father."[473] And again, "... All authority in Heaven and on Earth has been given to me."[474] Furthermore, *the Father loves the Son and has given all things into His hand.*[475]

For the apostle Paul, this was a present reality. He addresses Christ as "The King of Ages, immortal, invisible, the only God."[476]

Zechariah saw into a day when this rule would be *manifest* and *seen.* His prophecy says that, "the Lord will become King over all the Earth; on that day the Lord will be one and His name one."[477] The issue at hand is not God's rulership, but rather His show of power. This outward *display* of an ever-present rulership is the thing we are progressively seeing and tak-

---

[473] Luke 10:9, DAR
[474] Matt. 28:18, NIV
[475] John 3:35, ESV
[476] 1 Tim. 1:17, ESV
[477] Zech. 14:9, NRSV

ing part in. But that era of manifestation began and was summed up with Christ's work on the cross. It is sealed in His triumphant return.

> *Which in His times He **shall show**, who is the blessed and only Potentate, the King of kings, and Lord of lords.*[478]

+ The Nature of His Dominion

Two equally important principles that I wish to convey here are Christ's *present* dominion in the Earth and the *nature* of that dominion. His present kingship enables us to have authority now in earthly matters. The *nature* of that kingship means we don't wield our power in the *same way* that the world does.

Christians should have no problem owning billions of dollars. And they should have no problem giving it away.

His Kingdom consists of *real* ownership, but it is not greed-based. It consists of *real* reigning, but it is not fear-based. His authority is not based on fear, but rather He will have troops who volunteer freely in the day of His power.[479] There are no conscripts in the Lord's army, only free men.

He rules His government by a rod of iron, indeed! But this is only to keep the wolves away from His children. In the same note, His rule is more liberating than any democratic society we have ever known.

[478] 1 Tim. 6:15, AKJV

[479] See Ps. 110:3

More personally empowering than any earthly constitution or Magna Carta could fathom. The highest ideals of democracy, communism and socialism combined could not fathom the utopia of a monarchy ruled by this King. It is a society unlike any political dreamer could imagine.

The two witnesses' sphere of influence is figuratively Sodom and Egypt.[480] Egypt represents the oppression and control of corrupt government – that which enslaves God's people. Sodom represents licentiousness, rebellion and moral corruption. Control produces rebellion. Rebellion requires and incites control. Sodom and Egypt are a double cord of darkness found in every earthly kingdom from Rome to Babylon. But never do they thrive better than in the spheres of religion, which is why the two witnesses are located somehow literally in Jerusalem, "that great city ... where also their Lord was crucified."[481]

Neither control nor rebellion are found in this Kingdom of bliss. For the King and Kingdom are inseparable.

+ The Grace Grace Generation

Revelation 1:6 tells us again that we are a "Kingdom of priests." We are declaring a word of reconciliation between Heaven and Earth. We're proclaiming by the inexhaustible power of a complete and sevenfold unction the good news of Christ's finished work. The seven eyes of the Lord do not just range throughout

---

[480] See Rev. 11:8

[481] See Rev. 11:8

an intangible, unseen heavenly kingdom. They range *throughout the Earth*.

There are believers who will emerge in these days who possess billions and can raise the dead. The patriarchs of old were made famous both for their *natural* authority and *spiritual* authority. Abraham owned the riches of more than five kingdoms. But this *friend of God* was also able to heal an entire nation's physical barrenness with one prayer. When the spiritual and natural orders are in cohesion, it is fertile ground for the miraculous, freedom from poverty, righteous living, healthy homes and happy holiness. Governments are righteous. Pollution and disease are eradicated from society. The perfect cohesion of Eden is restored. The fulfillment of all our dreams comes from our boast in the great grace of Christ's reconciliatory work.

Zechariah saw two olive trees, but only one lampstand. John the Revelator saw two trees but *two lampstands*. The church is fully grafted into Israel's promises. But not all of the Jews have been grafted into the church. I do think there is coming a day when all of natural Israel will come into the saving knowledge of Messiah. I think this will be a prophetic signpost of a larger picture. It represents the entire natural order fully displaying a current spiritual reality.

These two trees and two lampstands represent a harmony between the spiritual and the natural, between the two covenants, between Heaven and Earth, between Jew and Gentile – between God and man. They represent a Kingdom flowing in complete union with God in Christ.

> *For if, by the trespass of the one man, death reigned through that one man, how much more will those who receive* ***God's abundant provision of grace*** *and of the* ***gift of righteousness reign in life*** *through the one man, Jesus Christ.*[482]

Kingdom authority is yours now to *reign in life*. And it is effortlessly based on the grand accomplishment of Him. It is not by might, nor by power, but *by His Spirit*.

+ Keeper of the Flame

The church age is about to awaken to the concept that our relationship with God is not based on self-effort, but on the inexhaustible grace of Christ's cross. These seven Spirits are the oil of Christ's grace flowing and burning through the church life. In the Old Testament, the priest was in charge of continually keeping the fires burning on the lampstand. It was a repetitive, laborious task. It took a lot of effort to stoke the old fires and maintain a life in the light of God.

But now, we have a new High Priest who has made a sacrifice once and for all. It is no longer your job to refill your lamps. You have a continual source of oil flowing from the cross – the *true olive tree* – that bubbles up from the inside of you. It requires no human maintenance.

In how many ways has the Lord tried to show there is a limitless supply of oil for them that believe? It's the

---

[482] Rom. 5:17, NIV

very reason that the modern Jewish Hanukkah menorah has nine lamps instead of seven. Back in the inter-Testamental period before the birth of Christ, the temple had been defiled in a Syrian invasion. The Maccabees, a Jewish rebel army from which the Pharisees trace their roots, overthrew the invading Syrian forces. But when the Jews went to rededicate the temple, there was only enough consecrated olive oil to fuel the temple lampstand for *one day*. But the small jar of oil miraculously burned for eight days, providing enough time for more oil to be pressed and prepared. Today, the nine-branched lampstand is symbolic of that miraculous flask of oil that never ran out. But we know the nine lamps also represent the entire Trinity – Father, Son and the sevenfold Spirit.

Here is another peculiar miracle that regularly points to our effortless assistance in keeping this flame stoked. The Greek Orthodox church has gathered every year at the Church of the Holy Sepulcher in Jerusalem on Easter, where a miracle called the Uncreated Light has taken place annually since the 1500s. The church patriarch enters into the sepulcher every year as part of the annual celebration. He is frisked by both religious and police authorities to make sure he is carrying no matches or similar fire-starting instruments. He then enters what is traditionally thought to be the tomb of Christ. The tomb is also thoroughly checked for sparking agents on the day before and sealed with beeswax.

When the patriarch enters, a flash of light and a sound fills the entire outer room outside as candles instantly catch aflame all throughout the building – even those high above human hand reach are spontaneously ignited. For the first few minutes the flames are harmless to touch even when hands, faces or beards are immersed in them. Like clockwork, this marvel happens every year. It is mysterious indeed, but the name is apropos. Christ is truly our *Uncreated Light*. Our union with Him burns strong, without the help of human hands.

+ TEN VIRGINS

I hope this also helps you to better understand the parable of the ten virgins. For their story relates much to having the oil of the Spirit in our lamps. You are familiar with the parable in Matthew 25, so I will only paraphrase it here. A Bridegroom had prepared a feast, but was a long time in coming. Meanwhile, all the bridesmaids were sleeping, when He finally shows up in the middle of the night. They awoke and quickly trimmed their wicks. There were five foolish virgins who did not prepare for the Bridegroom's coming because they did not buy oil beforehand for their lamps. Five others were called *wise*, and they kept extra oil on hand for His appearance. When the Bridegroom suddenly showed up, the foolish ones ran frantically to purchase oil. The five wise ones went straight to the feast and were received there.

Those who had run to purchase oil were not admitted to the feast.

Many view this parable improperly along two lines. For starters, they think it endorses *paranoia* – to fear that you could miss out based on the whim of the moment. And the other wrong view is that it is *your job* to keep your lamp oiled. Neither of these is the point or focus of the parable.

There are two themes that we have missed in this parable that we should see in the light of grace. For one, we shouldn't call this the parable of the *wise virgins*, but rather the *trusting virgins*. They may have been wise, but their wisdom was not based in superior virtue. They had their own character flaws. If the unprepared ones were simply lazy, we could make an equal argument that the prepared ones were selfish and snappy. They refused to share their oil with the unprepared virgins. In other words, they didn't have oil just because they were *better people* – nor did they have a higher moral standard.

It was not based on preparedness alone that Christ received some and didn't admit others. Ultimately *all of them* had been invited beforehand to this feast. But the five wise virgins were the only ones who *trusted in the invitation*. They believed the invitation was valid, and therefore they got ready for it.

Getting oil is not hard work. Even the foolish ones got it in one night. Therefore, the *effort* put forth on behalf of the wise ones to get oil was not their virtue. Your efforts don't fill you with the oil of the Spirit. The trusting virgins actually *believed* in the promise, and were therefore prepared.

The issue at hand was not preparation, but *faith*. The trusting virgins saw beyond the apparent "delay" of the *Bridegroom's* return. Instead of just living as if His presence was a *future* reality, they trusted the invitation and lived as if He were already right here. It was as easy as keeping an extra bottle of oil on the shelf. Just because the Bridegroom was taking a little longer than expected did not cause them to waiver in their trust. They believed the good news that He was coming, so they kept oil on hand.

Faith was their virtue. Faith proved their wisdom.

The second point to this parable comes in the form of a question: *Who is to say the foolish virgins would have been turned away from the feast, simply because they lacked oil?*

The frantic rush to purchase their own oil showed the basic root of the problem for the foolish virgins: *a propensity toward self-effort instead of simple trust.* They immediately ran to the world's trading floor, instead of marriage feast. Had the virgins simply gone directly to the Bridegroom at His appearing, I do not for a moment think they would have been turned away. In fact, following verses would have applied:

> *If you are wise you will get* ***from me*** *gold tested by fire, so that you may have true wealth; and white robes to put on, so that your shame may not be seen; and* ***oil for your eyes, so that you may see.***[483]

And again, "Come, all you who are thirsty, come to the waters; and you who have no money, come, buy ... *without money and without cost.*"[484]

---

[483] Rev. 3:18, BAS

[484] Isa. 55:1, NIV

Obtaining oil is not a matter of prayer, study, discipline or outward obedience. Rather, it is about turning to the Lord empty handed and confessing a continual dependence on His cross as our life source. Have you owned His cross as your own? Are you still trying to bear a cross that is separate from His, or have you realized that He has ultimately carried yours? Can you see that the two olive trees are one in the same? *For I have been crucified with Christ, I no longer live but Christ lives in me.*[485]

Your union with Christ was instant and effortless. You trusted the invitation. Now a limitless supply of inexhaustible oil runs through you – a sevenfold river.

Never think the point of this parable is about purchasing your own oil. Simon the Sorcerer fell into that trap. It's the bewitchment of religion that says you must earn this anointing. Some preachers will tell you that the anointing is expensive. That's right! It's worth far more than your whole life could purchase. It cost Christ *His* life.

The Bridegroom says that the moral of the story is "*stay awake.*"[486] What does that mean? Does it mean to never rest? Not only would that invalidate His nature as our Sabbath rest – it would also contradict the parable itself. I know Christians who are so hard on themselves they actually suffer sleep deprivation because they misunderstand this parable! All ten virgins fell asleep – that wasn't the problem. Five of those were still admitted.

---

[485] See Gal. 2:20

[486] See Matt. 25:13

Christ wants a church that is awake to the *remembrance* of His sacrifice. Awake to the reality that He is already here, even if you don't see Him yet. The almond tree of awakening is melded within this lampstand. Let us be ever reminded and trust in this invitation. It tells us that we are complete in wisdom, understanding, counsel, might, knowledge and the fear of the Lord.

Christ the King started His church and He has completed it. He has infused His people with His Spirit without measure. How can we manifest this unless we believe? And how can we believe unless we have heard?

You are commissioned and ordained with this inexhaustible oil of grace to preach the good news. If you have ever felt insignificant, powerless or facing insurmountable odds in this life, I would encourage you not to despise the day of small beginnings. Be rest assured that Christ has invested the full worth and weight of His Glory in you. These seven rejoice to see the plumb line in your hand. We are His triumphant, unstoppable church.

You carry a tangible, transferrable anointing resident within you that can tear down and uproot nations. Christ in you can overthrow principalities and heal the sick with your shadow. Power and might, wisdom and knowledge emanate from within you – untold treasure in an earthen vessel.

+ SEVEN WELLS OF GRACE

We read in Genesis that Isaac – the son of laughter – reopened the wells dug by His father Abraham. He also dug new ones. He opened a total of seven wells. Christ the Son has opened the sevenfold dayspring of the Father to us.

One of Abraham's most significant wells was at Beersheba. *Beersheba* means "well of sevens" and alternatively, "well of the oath" or "well of promise."[487] As the story goes, Abraham swears an oath to nearby ruler Abimelech that he will deal truthfully and amicably with him. Abraham next complains to Abimelech that some of his men had seized a well that belonged to Abraham.

> *But Abimelech said, "I don't know who has done this. You did not tell me, and I heard about it only today." So Abraham brought sheep and cattle and gave them to Abimelech, and the two men made a treaty. Abraham set apart* ***seven ewe lambs from the flock****, and Abimelech asked Abraham, "What is the meaning of these seven ewe lambs you have set apart by themselves?"*
>
> *He replied, "Accept these seven lambs from my hand as a* ***witness*** *that I dug this well." So that place was called Beersheba, because the two men swore an oath there.*[488]

Abraham gave seven lambs as a witness to the well. The seven lambs were the substance of a covenant. It

---

[487] Strong, *Exhaustive Concordance of the Bible*, See entries 875, 7651, 7650, 7649 and 7653.

[488] Gen. 21:26-31, NIV

was the "sevenfold lamb" of the covenant that kept the wells open for Abraham.

This entire passage is a shadow of the fullness of Christ sealing a covenant and opening the fullness of His seven wells of grace to us. The promise of the Father was opened by the Son.

Additionally, the word *sheba* from Beersheba, is closely related to a number of Hebrew words that mean "fullness, abundance, satisfaction, overabundance, a state of satiation or being overstuffed!"[489]

Are you fully satiated on Christ? Or are you looking for something more? On the cross, He sealed an agreement that you would be continually, abundantly satisfied with His overflowing presence. In fact, that you would be *overstuffed* with God!

Abraham planted a tamarisk tree in Beersheba, a symbol of the cross,[490] and later, in Isaac's day, the son also made a peace treaty with Abimelech, followed by a great feast of eating and drinking. This represented a second and future covenant. A covenant not of fasting, but of feasting!

The work of the cross has opened an abundant, overflowing, manifold well of satisfaction to us! We now continually feast on this sevenfold overflow of grace.

+ The Seven Words

---

[489] Warren Baker and Eugene Carpenter, ed., *The Complete Word Study Dictionary: Old Testament* (Chattanooga, TN: AMG Publishers, 2003), 1094-1095.

[490] See Gen. 21:34

A sevenfold offering was common in covenantal affairs. Seven victims were required to atone for a broken covenant in 2 Sam. 21. Levites were to offer seven types of sacrifices (oxen, sheep, goats, pigeons, wheat, oil and wine). And blood had to be sprinkled seven times before the Lord in front of the curtain that Christ would one day come to rend.[491] Likewise, the tabernacle itself carried seven chief utensils.

As we have noted, the words for *oath* and *taking an oath* both incorporate the number seven. Seven victims were slain, "especially at the ratification of a treaty, the notion of seven being embodied in the very term signifying to swear, literally meaning to *do seven times*." To this end, the number seven "appears in cases where the notion of satisfaction is required, as in reference to punishment for wrongs ... or to forgiveness of them."[492]

In the climactic throes of death, our Lord uttered what scholars call "The Seven Words" as He hung upon the cross. Here, in no particular order, are the last seven sayings of Christ as He hung on the tree.

The First Word:
"Father, forgive them for they do not know what they do."[493]
The Second Word:
"Today you will be with Me in Paradise."[494]

---

[491] See Lev. 4:6

[492] Hackett, *Smith's Dictionary of the Bible*, Vol. IV, 2935.

[493] See Luke 23:34

[494] See Luke 23:43

The Third Word:
"Woman, behold your son ... behold your mother."[495]
The Fourth Word:
"My God, My God, why have You forsaken Me?"[496]
The Fifth Word:
"I thirst"[497]
The Sixth Word:
"It is finished."[498]
The Seventh Word:
"Father, into Your hands I commend My spirit."[499]

In each of these words, we see the paramount themes of forgiveness, completion, reconciliation and restoration to the heavenly abode. We see His divinity and humanity. We see provision of a perfect sacrifice and perfect love embodied here.

"The progressive stages by which (these words) are characterized may be interpreted as showing a gradual unfolding of the will of God for the redemption of mankind," write professors John Davis and Henry Gehman.[500]

Here, He poured out the fullness of Himself.

+ OIL OF GRACE

---

[495] See John 19:26-27
[496] See Matt. 27:46
[497] See John 19:28
[498] See John 19:30
[499] See Luke 23:46
[500] Davis and Gehman, ed., *The Westminster Dictionary of the Bible*, 546.

SONS OF GOLDEN OIL

As a people who long to walk and operate in the full *charisma* of God's Spirit – let us never forget the center, source and focus of His presence and power.

It flows freely from Him.

The slain Lamb is the origin and destination of all that God is. His golden oil flows generously and without reserve to all who wish to drink. It comes from Him, burns effortlessly through us, and shines right back to Him. He alone is the starting point, the center and the finish mark. The Alpha and Omega in the salvation of men.

As much as men have worked through the course of history to take hold of the anointing, a generation of gospel purists is on the rise. A people who remember that the very word *charisma* doesn't mean "something to work up." Rather, it means "a gift of God's grace."

Our striving to be filled with the Spirit has been the very thing that has isolated us from it. Let Christ again be declared the only fountainhead of grace and the triumphal boast of His church. We will boast in no efforts but His. He is the Giver and the Gift.

For from Him and through Him and to Him are all things. To Him be the Glory forever! Amen.

+ About The Author

John Crowder and his wife, Lily, have a passion to spread the supernatural gospel of Jesus Christ in its exuberant love and joy. They have four children. The Crowders are revivalists based in Santa Cruz, CA. where they have planted a thriving local church community with friends. As founders of Sons of Thunder Ministries and Publications, they speak at events around the world. Along with thousands of articles, John has authored four books:

The New Mystics
The Ecstasy of Loving God
Mystical Union
Seven Spirits Burning

John and Lily long to release a creative new movement of ecstatic believers, who are enthralled by the finished works of Christ and who demonstrate miraculous lifestyles. Their heart is to see the Kingdom of God invade every sector of society. John has a vision to equip a supernatural generation to walk in the Glory – clearly communicating the finished work of the cross and operating in signs, wonders and the wine of divine intimacy needed for the last-day harvest.

Sons of Thunder plants children's homes for orphans and hosts evangelism campaigns, conferences and schools across the globe. John's ministry is marked by creative miracles and unusual signs and wonders.

+ Connect With Us

There are many ways to stay connected with us!

Visit us online at:
WWW.THENEWMYSTICS.COM

Find out about conferences, mission trips, schools, teaching resources, John's itinerary and more.

Email us at:
info@thenewmystics.org

Write us at:
P.O. Box 3591
Santa Cruz, CA 95063

Call us toll-free:
1-877-343-3245

Subscribe to John Crowder's magazine, *The Ecstatic*
www.TheNewMystics.com/Ecstatic

Visit us live at ***The Santa Cruz Church***
www.thesantacruzchurch.com

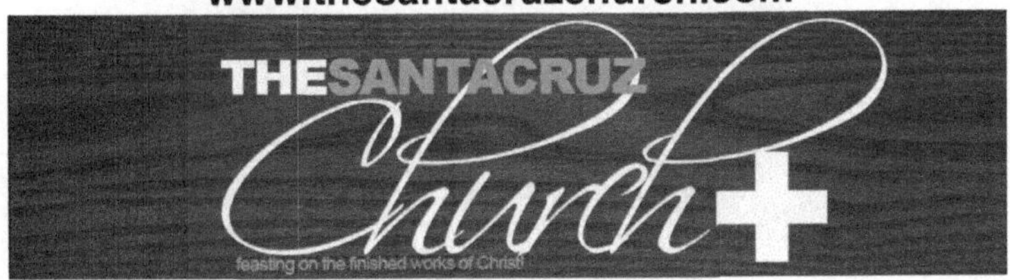

+ Free Weekly Teaching

Subscribe to *The Jesus Trip* ... a weekly video teaching on YouTube from John Crowder. You can join simply by visiting our web site: **www.TheNewMystics.com**. On our homepage, type in your email address and sign up for our weekly newsletter. You'll receive new video links every time they become available.

Or visit: **www.TheNewMystics.com/TheJesusTrip**

Have an iPhone? Get The New Mystics App for videos on the go!

+ More Books From The Author

The New Mystics

The supernatural generation

Two thousand years of miracle workers and pioneers crammed into one generation. The fiery bowls of heaven are being poured out through an extreme body of spiritual forerunners. Are you called to walk among them?

Miracle Workers, Reformers and the New Mystics contains more than 70 photos, illustrations, and biographies of men and women whose lives have demonstrated the phenomenal throughout the ages. Let their stories inspire you to join their ranks as part of this revival generation. **$16 + Shipping**

The Ecstasy of Loving God

Trances, raptures & the pleasures of Jesus Christ

God has destined you to live in the joyful radiance of Himself, just as Adam was called to live in the realm of Eden. Ecstasy, or "extasis," is the Greek term for trance, and is linked with a pleasurable, God-given state of out-of body experience recorded throughout the New Testament and the church age. In this book, John takes us on a journey from Old and New Testament ecstatic prophets to the future ecstatics who will usher in a massive wave of harvest Glory to the streets in these last days. **$20 + Shipping**

ORDER AT WWW.THENEWMYSTICS.COM
OR CALL TOLL-FREE 1-877-343-3245

NOTES